STARS ALL AROUND US

Quilts and Projects Inspired by a Beloved Symbol

By Cherié Wagner Ralston

Kansas City Star Books

Acknowledgements

First and foremost, I want to thank my husband John. Your love and support for 31 years has sustained me. This book wouldn't exist without you by my side.

Thanks to my children, Amy, John Charles and Joe. You are my world. You've put up with a lot of pins in your feet over the years!

My sewing group, The Women Who Run with Scissors, is a great group of women. Alma Allen, Barbara Brackman, Shauna Christensen, Pam Mayfield, Karla Menaugh, Deb Rowden, Jean Stanclift and Terry Thompson – thanks for your encouragement, caring and listening.

Thank you Lori Kukuk! Your awesome quilting makes my quilts shine. You are an artist!

Doug Weaver, thank you for this opportunity to show my work. Thanks also for spontaneously coming up with the name for the book!

Deb Rowden, my editor. Your patience is unbelievable. Thanks so much for all you did to get this book to publication. I will miss those editorial meetings! Deb also provided the star stories that begin every quilt chapter.

Eric Sears' illustrations are excellent. You understood me and made everything amazingly clear.

Jo Ann Groves provided wonderful art production support.

Vicky Frenkel, my book designer, thank you for your creative suggestions and fabulous work!

Jon Blumb, your beautiful photography brings my work to all to see. My thanks for helping with photography goes to: Alma Allen, Deb Rowden, and Sally Morrow.

Stars All Around Us
Quilts and Projects Inspired by a Beloved Symbol

Author: Cherié W. Ralston

Editor: Deb Rowden
Designer: Vicky Frenkel
Photography: Jon Blumb
Art illustration: Gary Embrey Design/Eric Sears
Production assistance by Jo Ann Groves

Published by:
Kansas City Star Books
1729 Grand Blvd.
Kansas City, Missouri, USA 64108

First edition, first printing

ISBN 0-9764021-2-2

Printed in the United States of America by Walsworth Publishing Co., Marceline, MO

To order copies, call StarInfo at (816) 234-4636 and say "Books." Or go to www.PickleDish.com

The Quilter's Home Page

TABLE OF CONTENTS

INTRODUCTION

We all have our obsessions. Cherié Ralston's is stars.

She notices them. Once she points them out, you can't help but notice them too.

You'll see them throughout this book: views of the stars all around us, some that Cherié passes every day.

You'll see them in her quilts and her projects.

Cherié has always liked stars (note what she's holding in her baby picture). She didn't realize how many stars she was surrounded by until she dreamed up this book. One day she pulled out her book of quilt designs at stitch group and everyone exclaimed, "They're all stars!"

And as you'll see in the following pages, they are. Cherié went home and took note of how many stars were all over her house. She had been collecting them for a long time.

Folk art stars hang on the front porch of her historic home in Lawrence, Kansas. They're etched on her wine glasses. Her charm bracelets jangle with stars, as do her earrings and necklaces.

"It's a weird little quirky thing I've got going. I'm really attracted to stars. I always notice them," she admits. Five pointed stars are her personal favorite.

Perhaps this all began for Cherié when she was growing up in the desert of Nevada, where the huge night sky twinkles with stars. Marriage to a physicist meant living in many places, but happily they have settled in a state, appropriately, with the motto of "To the stars through difficulty."

If you take note, you will see stars all around. The stars that twinkle down at us from the skies have been a comfort throughout the ages. You find them in folklore and history, in poems and songs, in paintings and on signs. You drive down roads named after stars and swim in lakes bearing their name.

All of the quilts and projects that follow have stars in them. We've included some stories about stars and some pictures of stars that have caught the eye of Cherié and her friends as they travel about.

There are patterns and instructions for **seven quilts**. Most feature some combination of pieced and appliqué designs, with easy-to-follow assembly instructions.

There are patterns and instructions for **four- teen projects**. They cover the range of Cherié's favorite creative pursuits other than quilts. If you hook rugs or do punchneedle embroidery, here are new designs for you. There are also lessons for creating a variety of book covers and even a painted sewing box.

The **lessons** at the back of the book include valuable tips about doing invisible machine ap- pliqué, and ways to cover any book. Cherie is the person many quilters turn to as they try to make quilt blocks fit together. She provides her own lessons for figuring out some of the **simple math** that simplifies quilt design work. Her lessons are valuable resources. Cherié also keeps a sharp eye out for timesaving products and she shares some of her favorites in her **Sources** at the back of the book.

Cherié has always been inspired by stars. The Kansas City Star, which also appreciates "star" power, is proud to bring her talents to you in this first "stars" book by Kansas City Star Quilts. Turn the page and enjoy the stars she has created for you.

—Deb Rowden

EVENING STAR

CHAPTER 1

THE BRIGHTEST STAR

The evening star is not a star at all. It is a planet that becomes visible in the western sky shortly after sunset (or in the eastern sky just before sunrise). We see it clearly in twilight, when it is too light for true stars to be seen. Venus and Mercury are often the evening stars we see. Other planets, especially Mars and Jupiter, may also appear as evening or morning stars at certain points in their orbits.

Venus reigns in brightness among stars and planets. Only our Sun and Moon outshine it.

It inspires poets. Edgar Allen Poe penned a famous poem titled Evening Star, as did Henry Wadsworth Longfellow and William Blake.

Newspapers, motels, roads, movies, camping resorts, paintings, cafes—even a few saloons—bear its name.

Cherié Ralston
Evening Star Road in western Johnson County, Kansas.

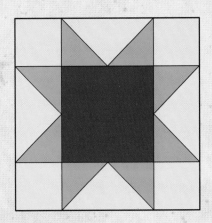

EVENING STAR

Block size: 8" (25 blocks needed)
Quilt size: 83" x 83"

Fabric Requirements:

- 25 fat quarters of beige backgrounds for blocks and sawteeth
- 25 fat quarters of a variety of dark colors for blocks, sawteeth and appliqué (including 3 greens, 3 reds and 3 purples)
- 1 yard red for setting squares
- 5/8 yard brown for setting triangles
- 1/3 yard dark brown for stop border
- 2 1/3 yards dark beige for appliqué border
- 5/8 yard green for vine and leaves
- 5/8 yard red for binding

From each beige background, cut:

• A: 2 – 5 1/4" squares.

Set one aside for flying geese border.

• B: 1 –5" square, cut into quarters
2 1/2" x 2 1/2".

A   A   B

From each dark, cut:

• C: 2 – 5 3/4" squares, cut into quarters
2 7/8" x 2 7/8".

Set four aside for flying geese border.

• D: 1 – 4 1/2" square.

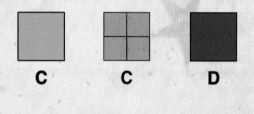

C   C   D

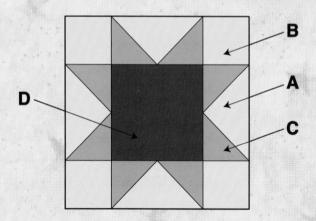

• Draw diagonal lines on the wrong side
of the 4 - 2 7/8" squares (C).

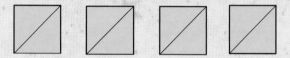

• Place 2 of these dark squares on opposite
corners of the background square (A),
right sides together, lining up drawn lines
diagonally. Sew 1/4" on each side of the
drawn lines.

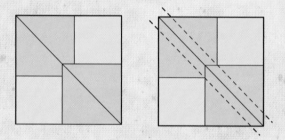

• Cut apart on the drawn line. Press open.

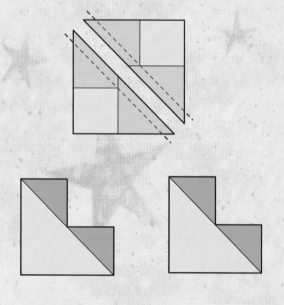

- Place a dark square on the corner of the large triangle, right sides together, making sure the drawn diagonal line runs from the corner to the center.

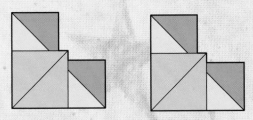

- Sew 1/4" on each side of the drawn line. Do this on both pieces.

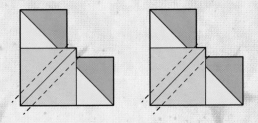

- Cut apart on the drawn lines. Press open.

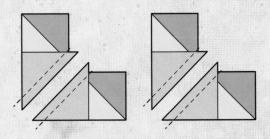

- This will yield 4 flying geese units.

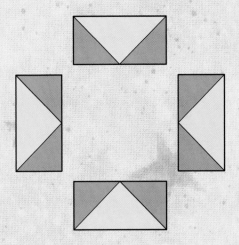

Assemble the blocks as shown:

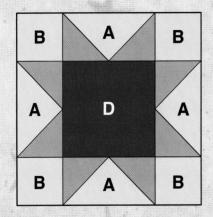

Make 25 blocks using this method. For added interest when assembling the blocks, use different background fabrics for A and B in some of the blocks. This will give your quilt more of an antique look.

Setting your blocks:

1. Setting squares.

From 1 yard of red fabric, cut 16 –
8 1/2" x 8 1/2" squares.

2. Setting side triangles.

From 5/8 yard of brown fabric, cut 4 –
12 5/8" x 12 5/8" squares. Cut in quarters
diagonally.

3. Setting corner triangles.

Cut 2 – 6 1/2" x 6 1/2" squares.
Cut in half diagonally.

Stop border:

- From 1/3 yard dark brown, cut 6 -1 1/2"
  strips. Seam these strips together to make
  one long strip.
- From this, cut 2 strips 1 1/2" x 56 1/2".
  Attach one to each side.
- Cut 2 strips 1 1/2" x 58 1/2". Attach one
  to the top and one to the bottom.

Appliqué border:

From the 2 1/3 yards border fabric, cut:

- 2 strips 10 1/2" x 58 1/2".
  Attach one to each side.

- 2 strips 10 1/2" x 78 1/2".
  Attach one to the top and one to the
  bottom.

From the remaining fabric, cut:

- 23 large berries
- 43 small berries
- 16 small stars
- 4 large stars
- 4 medium stars
- 40 large leaves
- 40 medium leaves
- 40 small leaves

Bias vine:

- From the 5/8 yard green fabric, cut 9 yards
  of 1 1/2" bias strips for the vine. Sew these
  strips together into one long strip. Pull this
  strip through a Clover bias tape maker #18
  (to make 3/4" bias).

- Also cut 2 yards of 1" bias vine. Seam these
  strips together into one long strip. Pull this
  strip through a Clover bias tape maker #12
  (to make 1/2" bias).

Referring to photo, arrange vines, leaves, stars
and berries on the border. Appliqué.

Flying geese border:

- This uses the 25 - 5-1/4" squares that you cut previously and set aside and the 25 - 5 3/4" squares, cut into quarters 2 7/8" x 2 7/8".
- Use the same flying geese method that you used for the stars to assemble the flying geese border.

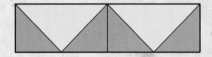

Stars peek out a front porch on Pennsylvania Street in Lawrence.

- Sew units together into 2 strips of 19. Attach one to each side of the quilt.
- Sew 2 more strips with 20 units. Attach one to the top and one to the bottom.

Final border:

- From the 5/8 yard red fabric, cut 9 strips 2" x width of fabric (approximately 44" wide).
- Trim off selvedges.
- Sew these strips together end to end to make one long strip.
- From this strip, cut 2 strips 2" x 80 1/2". Attach to one each side.
- Cut 2 more strips 2" x 83 1/2". Attach one to the top and one to the bottom.

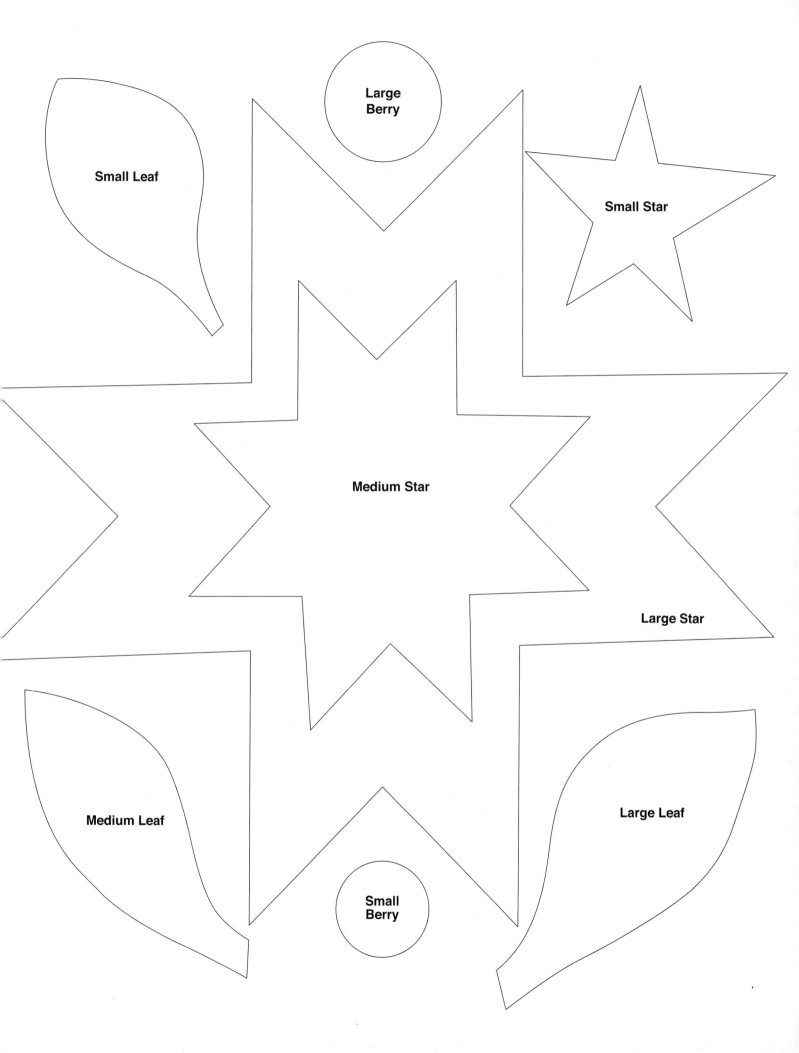

STARDUST

CHAPTER 2

REMNANTS OF STARS

Stardust can be romantic or scientific, depending on which definition you use:

• A cluster of stars too distant to be seen individually, resembling a dimly luminous cloud of dust.

• The remnants of the death of stars, the most ancient meteorite material, older than the solar system itself.

• A dreamy romantic or sentimental quality.

According to a team of German physicists, all life on our planet had its origins in stardust, which probably brought the microscopic building blocks of life to Earth billions of years ago. They estimate about 4,000 tons of interstellar dust fall to Earth each year, although most of it vaporizes in the atmosphere.

Our Stardust is a medallion quilt. The center square is alive with an inviting home, shaded by a tree and the moon. The border is filled with six-pointed stars.

Look around and you'll find stars everywhere, like the ones carved into the gingerbread decoration above the entrance to this house, above.

Cherié Ralston
A starry front porch in Eudora, Kansas.

STARDUST

Quilt size: 50" x 50"

Fabric requirements:

- 2/3 yard gold for center
- 6" x 9" bright gold for windows
- 9" x 4" black for roof
- 7" x 10" blue for tall part of house
- 7" x 7" blue for main part of house
- 1 fat quarter brown for tree trunk
- 7" x 7" cheddar for stars
- 2 fat eighths green for leaves
- 1/2 yard medium beige for sawteeth and vine border
- 1 fat quarter blue for sawteeth
- 1/2 yard gold for vine border
- 1/4 yard 2 different reds for setting triangles
- 1/2 yard brown for setting triangles
- 1/4 yard of 5 different beige fabrics for 6 pointed star backgrounds
- 1/4 yard 5 different gold fabrics for 6 pointed stars

Center:

- From 2/3 yard gold fabric, cut **center square** 20 1/2" x 20 1/2".

- **Cut out and prepare appliqué shapes.** Follow the drawing for placement, baste in place. Appliqué.

Sawtooth border:

- From the beige fabric and the fat quarter of blue, **make a grid sheet** of 2 7/8" squares for 2" finished size sawtooth units. Mark 6 squares by 4 squares (see figure 1). This grid sheet will yield 48 sawteeth. For the border, you will only need 44 sawteeth. Refer to Chapter 18, *Making Half Square Triangles*, for detailed instructions of this method. Another way to make half square triangles is to use Triangles on a Roll™ (see source list at the back of the book).

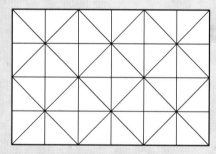

Fig 1

- Once the grid sheet is sewn, **cut apart on the drawn lines**, press toward the dark fabric and trim. Sew together 2 strips of 10 sawteeth, as shown in figure 2. Attach one strip to each side of the center block (see figure 4).

Fig 2

- Sew 2 strips of **12 sawteeth**. Note the different set of one block at each end (see figure 3). Attach one strip to the top and one to the bottom (see figure 4).

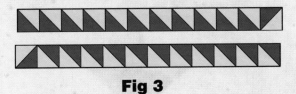

Fig 3

Fig 4

Vine border:

- From 1/2 yard gold, **cut 2 strips** 3 1/2" x 24 1/2". Attach one to each side of the quilt. **Cut 2 strips** 3 1/2" x 30 1/2". Attach one to the top and one to the bottom of the quilt.

- From medium beige, **make 4 yards** of 1/2" finished bias vine. To do this, cut bias

strips 1" wide and pull through a Clover™ bias tape maker #12.

- **Cut out 24 leaves.** Baste all in place, referring to the photo for placement, and appliqué.

Six pointed star border:

- From a variety of beige fabrics, cut 16 7 1/2" **squares**.

- From a variety of gold fabrics, cut 16 6-pointed **stars**. Baste in place and appliqué. Set aside.

- From the brown fabric, cut 3 **squares** 11 1/4". Cut in quarters diagonally. (*Note: refer to the How to Make Setting Triangles lesson at the back of the book.*)

- Cut **6 brown squares** 5 7/8". Cut in half diagonally.

- From the red fabric, cut **3 squares** 11 1/4". Cut in quarters diagonally.

- Cut **2 red squares** 5 7/8". Cut in half diagonally.

Attach **1 border to the top** and **1 to the bottom,** with the red triangles on the inside.

Assembling the border:

Make 2 as follows:

Attach **1 border to each side** of the quilt with the red triangles on the inside.

Make 2 more as follows:

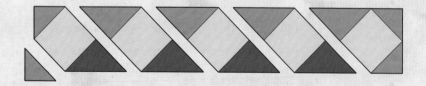

Placement Diagram-25%

C

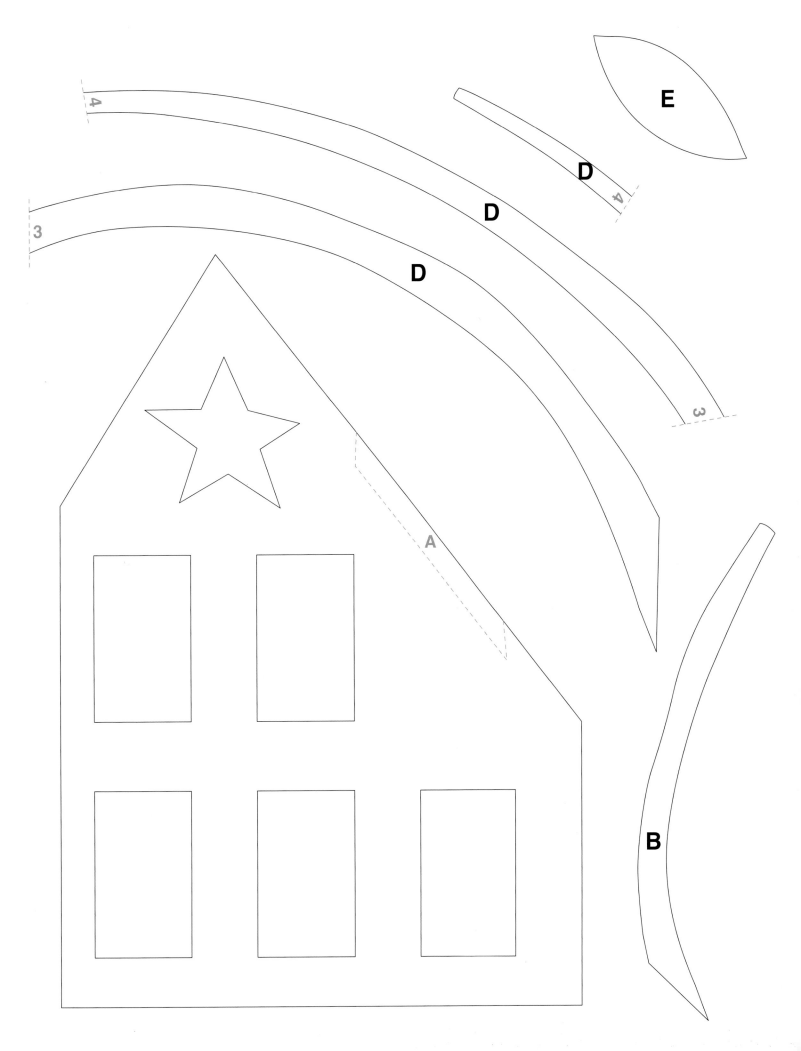

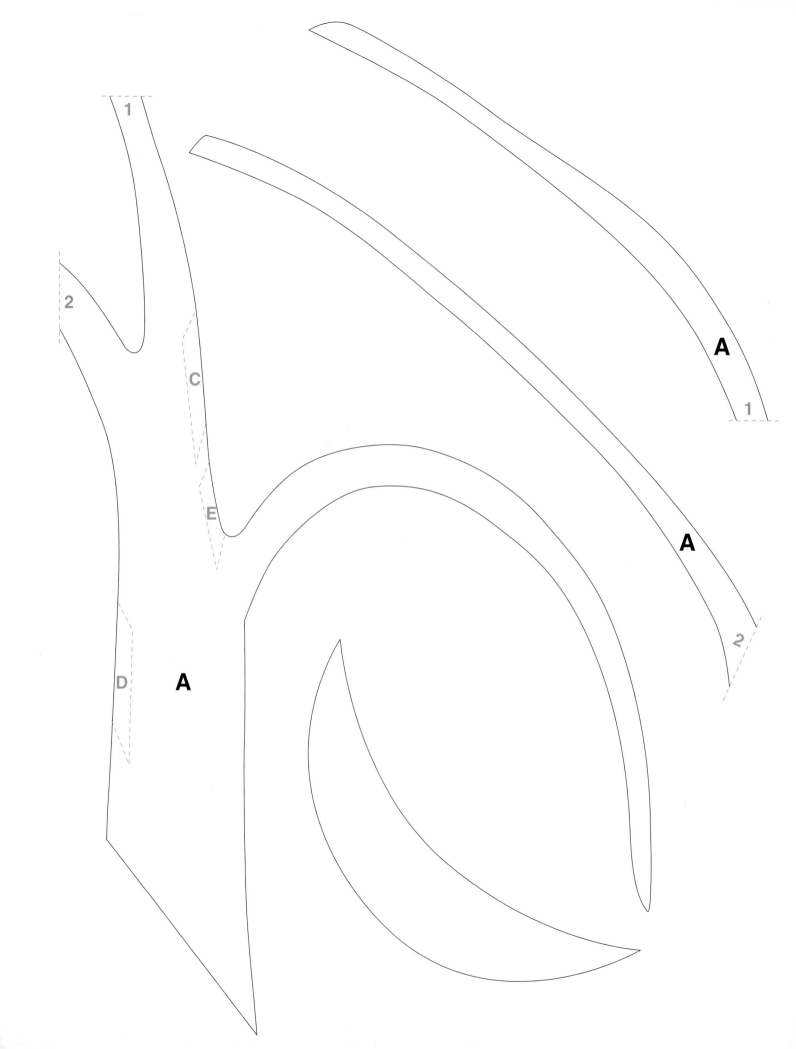

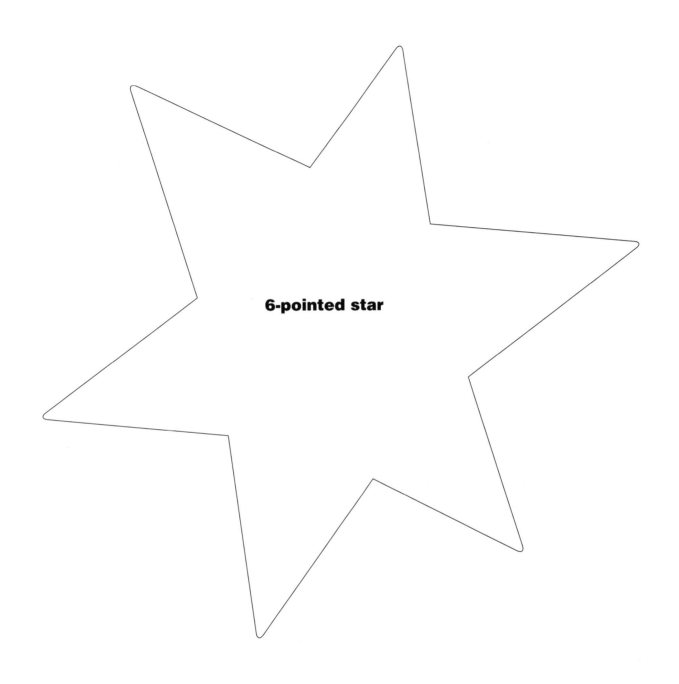

6-pointed star

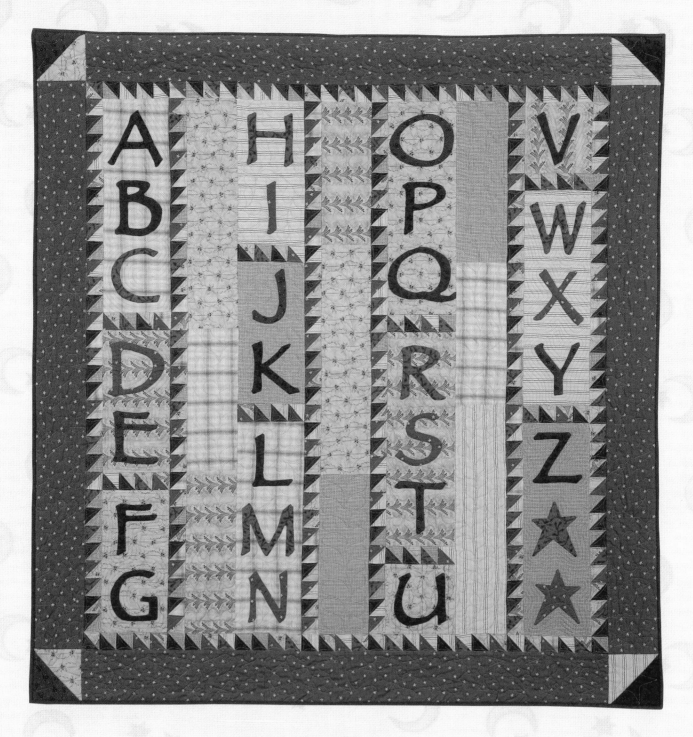

DREAMLAND

CHAPTER 3

SWEET DREAMS

Sweet dreams till sunbeams find you
Sweet dreams that leave all worries behind you
But in your dreams whatever they be
Dream a little dream of me.

—The Mamas and the Papas

Stars and dreaming go hand in hand. We wish our children sweet dreams when we tuck them in to bed. If you take note of hotels and motels on the back roads of America, you'll be surprised how many use stars and dreams in their names and signs. You can find homes away from home with names like the Starlite and the Dreamland Motel.

Stars offer mankind comfort. Their fixed positions in the skies have long guided travelers. The ancients lovingly regarded stars as living entities—heavenly angels, legendary heroes, the souls of the unborn and souls of the dead.

Deb Rowden
Route 36 travelers can stop at the Starlite Motel in Seneca, Kansas.

Barbara Brackman
A Dreamland Motel operates in Junction City, Kansas.

DREAMLAND

Quilt size: 55 1/2" x 57"

This baby quilt would look great in any color-way—greens, blues, soft pastels on a light background, or maybe light colors or pastels on a dark background. It's a nice big quilt for a baby, and it doesn't take that long to make.

Fabric requirements:

- 1 1/4 yards red print (for border, sawteeth and letters)
- 1/3 yard 4 more red prints (for sawteeth and letters)
- 5/8 yard 5 tan prints or plaids (for backgrounds and sawteeth)
- *Note: I numbered the fabrics for this quilt. Assign numbers to your 5 reds and 5 tans to follow the instructions below.*

Cutting:

(Note: all measurements include a 1/4" seam allowance, except for appliqué pieces.)

From each tan print cut:

- 1 strip 6 1/2" x width of fabric
- 1 strip 5" x width of fabric (set aside for setting strips)

From the 6 1/2" tan strips, cut:

#1 – cut 2 - 6 1/2" x 18 1/2"
#2 – cut 1 - 6 1/2" x 18 1/2"
        1 - 6 1/2" x 12 1/2"
        1 - 6 1/2" x 6 1/2"
#3 – cut 1 - 6 1/2" x 18 1/2"
        1 - 6 1/2" x 12 1/2"
        1 - 6 1/2" x 6 1/2"
#4 – cut 1 - 6 1/2" x 18 1/2"
        1 - 6 1/2" x 12 1/2"
#5 – cut 1 - 6 1/2" x 18 1/2"
        1 - 6 1/2" x 12 1/2"

Cut out red appliqué letters:

#1 – cut A, F, K, P, U, Z
#2 – cut B, G, L, Q, V, star
#3 – cut C, H, M, R, W, reverse star
#4 – cut D, I, N, S, X
#5 – cut E, J, O, T, Y

Referring to the quilt diagram, place letters on tan backgrounds and appliqué. Set aside.

Setting strips:

Using the 5" tan strip you cut previously, cut the setting strips:
#1 – cut 2 - 5" x 12 1/2"
#2 – cut 1 - 5" x 12 1/2"
        1 - 5" x 14"
#3 – cut 2 - 5" x 20"
#4 – cut 1 - 5" x 20"
#5 – cut 2 - 5" x 14"

Referring to the quilt diagram, piece into setting strips. Set aside.

Sawteeth:

You will need 274 – 1 1/2" finished sawteeth for this quilt.
- From the remaining 5 red and 5 tan fabrics, cut **7 red** and **7 tan** 4 3/4" squares from each. Pair one tan and

one red right sides together. This will make **35 square sets**. With a pencil, draw a diagonal line in both directions. Sew a 1/4" seam on either side of the drawn lines.

• Cut apart like this:

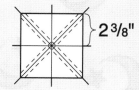

2 ³/₈"

(You can also use Triangles on a Roll™ (1 1/12" finished size) to make these sawteeth. See source list at the end of the book.)

• Press open towards the red. Trim off the points.

Assemble sawteeth strips as follows:

• Make **8 strips of 4 sawteeth.**

• Make **6 strips** for verticals (30 triangles).

• Make **1 for the top** and **1 for the bottom** (31 triangles).

• Assemble the quilt in strips, referring to the drawing for placement.

Final border:

• From the remaining largest piece of red fabric, **cut 5 strips** 5" x the width of the fabric. Trim off the selvedges. Seam these strips together end to end to make one long strip. Press. From this strip, cut 2 side strips 5" x 48 1/2".

• Cut the **top and bottom strips** 5" x 47".

• To make the corner triangle units, **cut 2 - 5 3/8" squares** each of tan and red. Place them right sides together. Draw a diagonal line and sew a 1/4" seam on either side of the drawn line.

- - - - - - -	= stitching line
——————	= cutting line

- **Cut apart** on the drawn line. Press toward the red fabric. Attach 1 to each end of the top and bottom strips.

- Sew the side borders to the body of the quilt. Press. Attach the top and bottom borders. Press.

Quilt Diagram
(numbers refer to background fabrics)

X = bottom of the letter

X = bottom of the letter

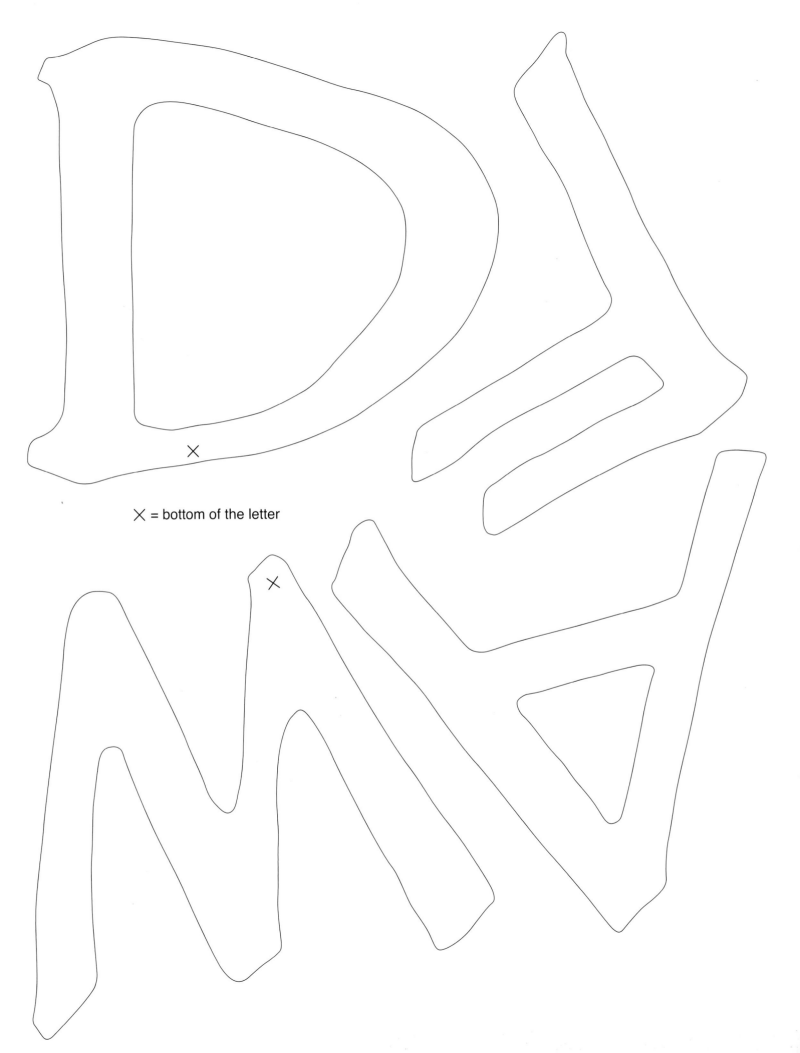

✕ = bottom of the letter

$\times$ = bottom of the letter

X = bottom of the letter

X = bottom of the letter

X

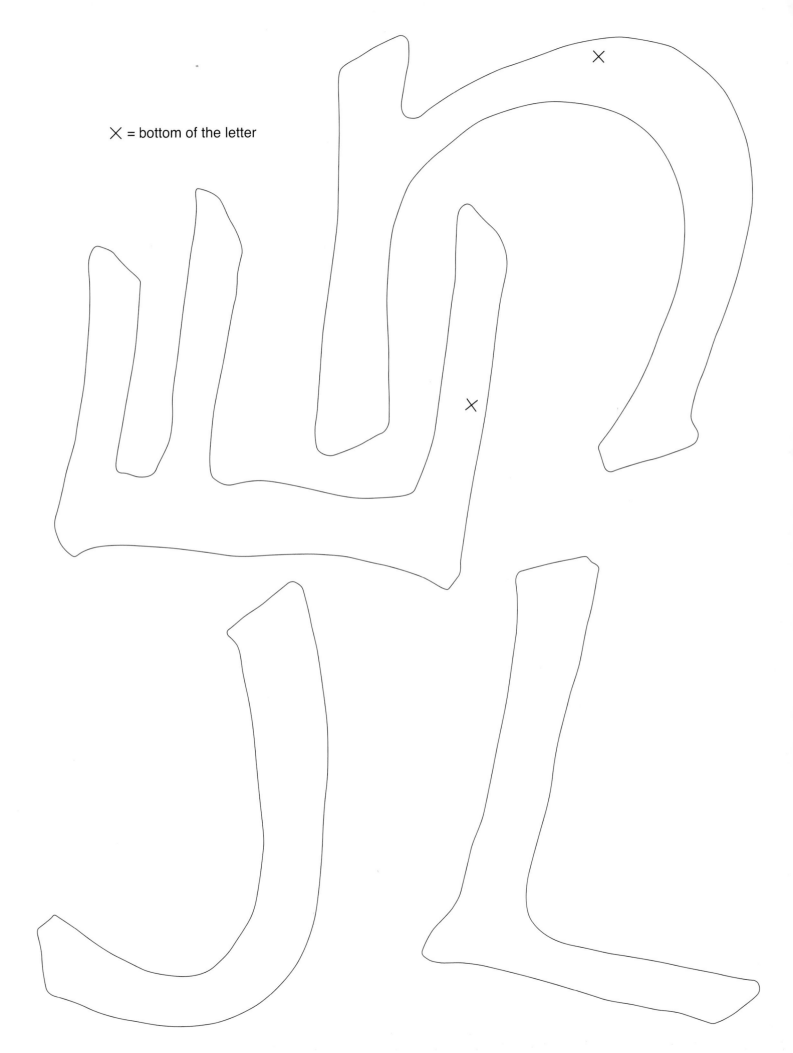

✕ = bottom of the letter

SWING ON A STAR

CHAPTER 4

FIVE-POINTED STARS

This design features a five-pointed star. Known also as a pentagram, pentangle, and pentacle, this symbol has many meanings. It's an endless line in a radial pattern, which can prove hypnotic. Such patterns have been credited with the power to repel evil forces, as well as to invite enlightenment from within.

Thanks to Betsy Ross, the American flag features a five-pointed star. George Washington's original sketch for the flag included six-pointed stars. Betsy demonstrated a simple way to fold fabric and cut a single snip to create her star and won the commission to make the first American flag.

Cherié Ralston
This star adorns an abandoned post office in the ghost town of Gold Hill, Nevada.

Slice an apple in half and you'll see a pentacle, called the star of knowledge by the gypsies. Other pentacles in nature are five petaled flowers like the apple blossom and the rose.

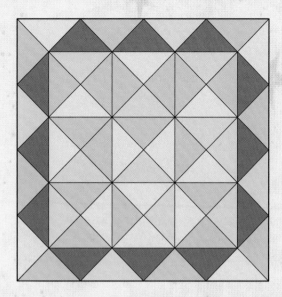

SWING ON A STAR

Block size: 20" x 20" (9 blocks needed)

Quilt size: 80" x 80"

I decided that it was time I had a Christmas quilt! The pieced backgrounds give the quilt added texture and richness. If you prefer, the appliqué could be done on non-pieced backgrounds. Either way, it makes a stunning quilt.

Fabric requirements:

- 2/3 yard of 7 different beige fabrics
- 1 fat quarter of 4 different greens
- 2/3 yard of 4 different reds

Preparing the background:

- From each beige background fabric, cut **2 squares** 21 1/4" x 21 1/4".

- **Cut in quarters**—corner to corner—in each direction. This will yield 56 large triangles.

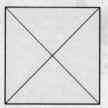

- **Set aside** 16 triangles for the border.

- Using 36 triangles, mix fabrics and sew together to form **9 - 20 1/2" squares** (unfinished size). There will be 4 remaining triangles. Save for another project.

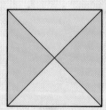

Preparing the applique:

- Using your favorite appliqué method, **cut 36** each of templates A, C, E, F, G and H from the green fabrics.

- From the red fabrics, **cut 36** each of templates B and D. Cut 9 of template I.

- Referring to the lines on the Placement Diagram, **arrange appliqué**. Appliqué all blocks.

Attaching the border:

- Attach a border strip to **each side** of the quilt body.

- Attach a border strip to the **top and bottom**. Finish by sewing the corner diagonal seams.

Assembling the blocks:

- Sew blocks together in **3 rows of 3**. Set aside.

Border:

- From the red fabrics, **cut 3 squares** 21 1/4" x 21 1/4". Cut in quarters diagonally in both directions.

- **Sew together** 4 beige and 3 red triangles as follows. Do this 4 times.

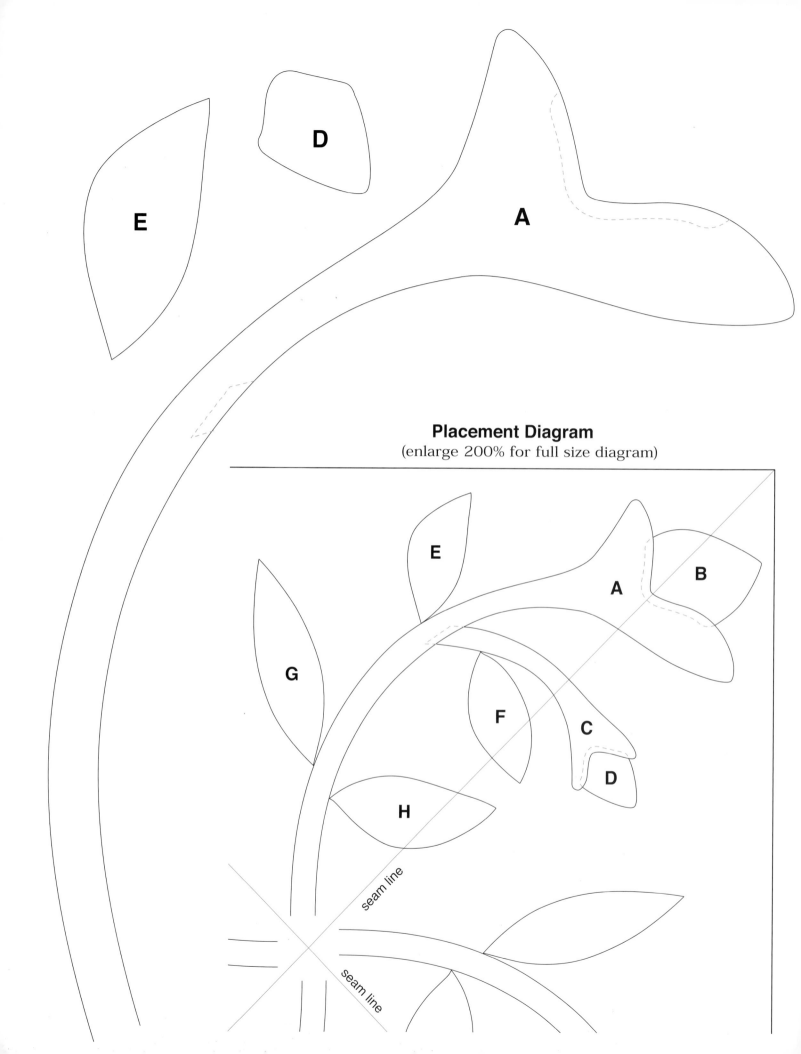

E

D

A

Placement Diagram
(enlarge 200% for full size diagram)

E

B

A

G

F

C

D

H

seam line

seam line

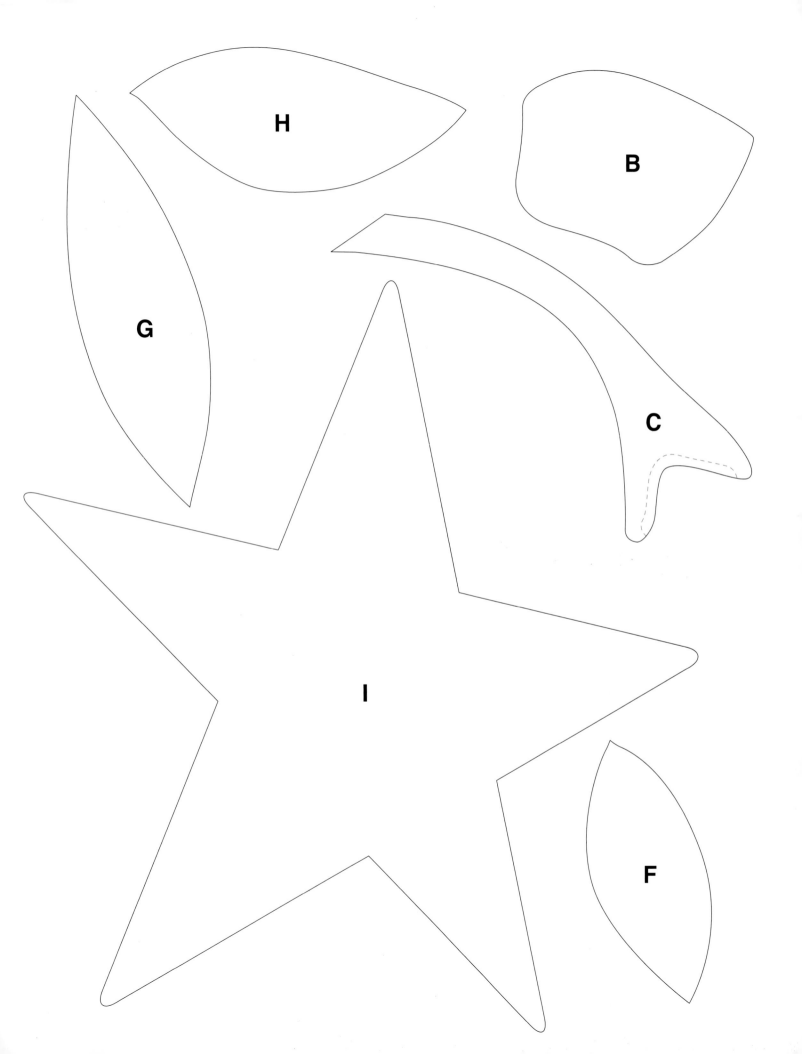

HARVEST SUN

CHAPTER 5

HARVEST SUN

Star quilts are revered in Native American culture. The quilts are a link to the past, to buffalo hides and war bonnets decorated with star designs.

Legend often made the roaming Morning Star a noble hunter. Morning Star and all the other star people were said to be super-human with powers only imagined by earthlings. The Blackfoot Indians allowed humans to marry stars in their tales. The lives of these humans were always tangled when they failed to understand the ways of the star people.

Today's treasured star quilts are often pieced diamonds, making six- or eight-pointed stars. The quilts are used in church ceremonies and as altar cloths. They are commemorative quilts for births, rites of passage and deaths. Quilts are the materials of choice because, as handmade objects, they represent an investment of time, thought, and self.

Cherié Ralston
Stars serve as shoe scrapers on this saloon threshold in Virginia City, Nevada.

HARVEST STAR

Block size: 24"

Quilt size: 88" x 88"

I used a freezer paper piecing method to assemble these suns. This method is fun and will give you nice sharp points.

Fabric requirements:

- 1/3 yard of 9 different lights (backgrounds and sawteeth)
- Fat quarters of 9 different pumpkins (centers and sawteeth)
- Fat quarters of 9 different rusts (petals and sawteeth)
- 1/3 yard of 9 different greens (outer backgrounds, vine and leaves)
- 2 1/8 yards medium pumpkin for border

Supplies:

- 2" finished Triangles on a Roll™
- Freezer paper

Freezer paper piecing
Preparing the freezer paper:

- Copy the freezer paper template page for the large sun (see page 53) 9 times (one copy for each block you are making).

- Stack 4 sheets of freezer paper—approximately 8 1/2" x 11"—for each sun block, shiny side up.

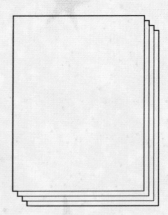

- Place 1 photocopy of the pattern on top of this stack.

- Press the tip of the iron on all marked x's to tack the pieces together. Depending on the heat of your iron, you may need to hold the tip in place for 1-3 seconds.

- On your cutting mat use, an x-acto knife and ruler to cut the pieces apart on all drawn lines. *Accuracy is very important.*

- Carefully pull the freezer paper apart.

- Cut 1 freezer paper center. Transfer the placement lines onto the freezer paper pattern. Set aside.

Preparing the fabric:

- Iron the shiny side of the freezer paper pattern **A** to the back of the light fabric, leaving approximately 1/2" between each piece.

- Iron the shiny side of the freezer paper pattern **B** to the back of the dark fabric, leaving approximately 1/2" between each piece.

- If the freezer paper comes loose at anytime while you are working, simply re-iron.

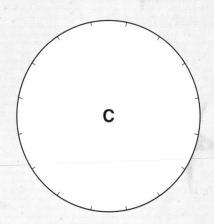

- Cut 4 freezer paper D templates. Transfer the placement lines onto the freezer paper patterns. Set aside.

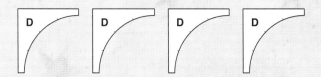

- With a rotary cutter and mat, trim each piece **adding a 1/4" seam allowance** on all sides. I use the Add-a-Quarter™ 1/4" ruler for this (see source list at the back of the book). The ledge on the ruler fits right up against paper and makes it easy and accurate to add the correct seam allowance.

- On the **inner and outer curves**, with a pencil of a color you can see, draw your seam line along the edge of the freezer paper. Cut with scissors or rotary cutter leaving a 1/4" seam allowance. Set aside.

- Iron the shiny side of the freezer paper center (**C**) to the back of the selected fabric. Transfer placement lines onto the seam allowance of the fabric. Also draw the seam line along the edge of the freezer paper. Cut out, leaving a 1/4" seam allowance. Remove the paper and set aside.

- Iron the shiny side of the freezer paper pieces D to the back of the selected fabric. Transfer placement lines onto the seam allowance of the fabric and draw the seam line along the inside curved edge of the freezer paper. Cut out, leaving a 1/4" seam allowance and remove the paper. Set aside.

Sewing the units:

- Pin piece **A** to piece **B**, matching points and lining up the edges of the fabric. This will automatically line up the paper edges. Stitch along the edge of the paper.

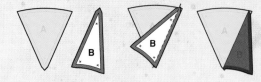

- Leave the paper in place on both **A and B pieces** and sew the seam from top to bottom. Do this for all 16 units in the block.

- Press all of the seams in the same direction.

- Pin these **A/B** units into pairs and sew the next seam. Leave all the freezer paper attached. If it comes loose, press again.

- Continue stitching until you have a ring of the **A/B** units. Leave the paper in (to keep fabric from stretching) and press. Once the ring is pressed, remove the paper.

- Matching the placement lines on the center circle to the inside points of the ring and pinning well, set in the center circle (**C**). If you prefer, you can appliqué the center circle onto the ring.

- Sew the 4 corner units (**D**) into one unit as shown.

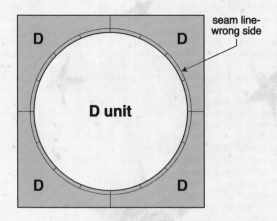

seam line-
wrong side

D unit

• To set the sun into the **D** unit, place the pieced sun on the table right side up. Place the **D** unit on top of the sun as shown. With right sides together, pin one of the points of the pieced sun to one of the placement lines on the **D** unit.

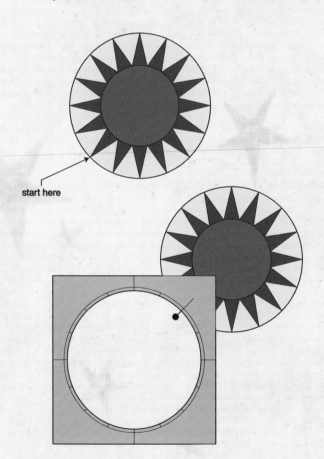

start here

• Move to the next sun point and **D** unit placement line. Continue until you have gone all the way around the sun.

• Now begin lining up the drawn seam lines that you made earlier on the **A** piece and the **D** piece. Place 2-3 pins between the pins that you have previously placed at the points. Continue all the way around.

• Sew on the drawn line, making sure to take out the pins as you come to them. Or, if you prefer, the sun may be appliquéd to the **D** unit. Press, being careful not to distort the block.

• Make 8 more sun blocks. Set aside.

Sawteeth (396 are needed):

• From each of the 9 different 1/3 yard light fabrics, **cut 2** rectangles 18" x 6".

• From each of the 9 different pumpkin fabrics and the 9 different rust fabrics, **cut 1** rectangle 18" x 6".

• Pair up each pumpkin and rust fabric rectangle with a light rectangle right sides together. Place a Triangles on a Roll™ strip that is 2 units x 6 units on top of each pair. Pin in place and sew as directed on the package.

• Cut apart, tear off the paper and press to the dark side. Trim points. *This will yield 24 finished sawteeth from each set of the 18 paired fabrics.*

Assembling the quilt:

- Make **36** units with 10 sawteeth each. ***Do not press***.* (*Note: not pressing lets you ease in any extra fullness when attaching.) Set aside 18 units.

- Make **18 - 2** unit sets of sawteeth. ***Do not press***.*

- Attach a 2 unit set to the right hand side of **18** of the 10 unit sets. This makes 18 – 12 unit sets.

Assemble the quilt center like this:

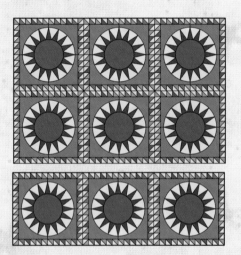

- Attach a 10 unit set to the sides of each sun block. Make sure the dark triangles are next to the block and that all seam allowances are turned in the same direction.

- Next, attach the 12 unit sets to the top and bottom of each block. Again, make sure that the dark triangles are next to the block and that all seam allowances are turned in the same direction. ***Do not press*** until all sawteeth are attached to each block. Do this for all 9 blocks.

Appliqué border:

- **Cut 104 leaves** from the remaining green fabrics. From four backgrounds, cut **4 large stars, 16 small stars and 24 berries.**

- From the 2 1/8 yards of border fabric, cut 4 strips 8 1/2" x 72 1/2". Press in half lightly to find the center. Next, press in half lightly lengthwise to mark the placement of the vine.

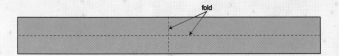

• Measure 3 1/2" from either side of the center fold to begin placing leaves. Place a pin to mark this point.

• Now measure every 5" for subsequent leaf placement. After the sixth leaf placement is marked, make another mark 2 1/2" away for the last leaf. Do this on both sides.

• Baste the vine in place.

• Place leaves with one end on the marks you have made at about a 45° angle. The other end of the leaf should be about 1" from the cut edge.

• Place the star in the center of the border. Baste in place.

• Place the berries and the small stars, referring to the photo. Baste in place.

Do this for all 4 borders. Appliqué all pieces.

Four corner suns:

• Copy the freezer paper template page for the four corner suns (see page 54). One copy will make all 4 blocks.

• Stack 4 sheets of freezer paper—approximately 8 1/2" x 11"—for each sun block, shiny side up.

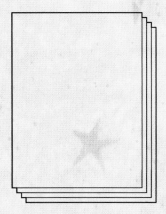

• Place 1 photocopy of the pattern on top of this stack.

• Press the tip of the iron on all marked x's to tack the pieces together. Depending on the heat of your iron, you may need to hold the tip in place for 1-3 seconds.

• On your cutting mat, use an xacto knife and ruler to cut the pieces apart on all drawn lines. *Accuracy is very important.*

• Carefully pull the freezer paper apart.

- Cut 1 freezer paper center G. Transfer the placement lines onto the freezer paper pattern. Set aside.

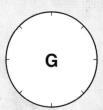

- Cut 4 freezer paper template **H**'s. Transfer the placement lines onto the freezer paper patterns.

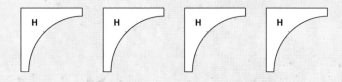

Preparing the fabric:

- Iron the shiny side of the freezer paper to the back of the selected fabric, leaving approximately 1/2" between each piece. Place **E** on the light fabric, **F** on the dark fabric. If the freezer paper comes loose at anytime while you are working, simply re-iron.

- Trim each piece, adding a 1/4" seam allowance. I use the Add-a-Quarter™ 1/4" ruler for this. The ledge on the ruler fits right up against paper and makes it easy to add the correct seam allowance.

- On the inner and outer curves, draw the seam line along the edge of the freezer paper. Cut out with scissors or rotary cutter, leaving a 1/4" seam allowance.

- Iron the shiny side of the freezer paper center (**G**) to the back of the selected fabric.

- Transfer placement lines onto the seam allowance of the fabric. Also, draw the seam line along the edge of the freezer paper.

- Cut out, leaving a 1/4" seam allowance. Remove paper and set aside.

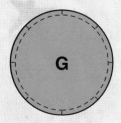

- Iron the shiny side of the freezer paper pieces **H** to the back of the selected fabric.

- Transfer placement lines onto the seam allowance of the fabric and draw the seam line along the inside curved edge of the freezer paper.

- Cut out, leaving a 1/4" seam allowance. Remove paper. Set aside.

Sewing the units:

- Pin piece **E** to piece **F** at the points and line up the edges of the fabric. This will automatically line up the paper edges. Stitch along the paper's edge.

- Leave the paper on both **E** and **F** pieces and sew the seam from top to bottom. Do this for all 8 units in the block.

- Press all of the seams in the same direction.

- Pin these units into pairs and sew the next seam. Leave all the freezer paper attached. If it comes loose, press it again.

- Continue adding units until you have a ring. Leave the paper on to keep the fabric from stretching and press. Remove the paper.

- Match the placement lines on the center circle to the inside points of the ring and pin well. Set in the center (**G**). If you prefer, you can appliqué the center circle onto the **E/F** ring.

- Sew the 4 corner units into 1 unit. Transfer the placement lines onto the fabric with a fine point pencil. Transfer the seam lines also. Remove the paper.

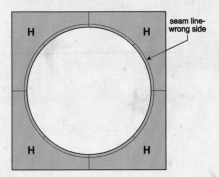

- To set the small sun into the **H** unit, place the small pieced sun on the table right side up. Place the **H** unit on top of the sun as shown, with right sides together. Line up a point on the sun with a placement line on the outer ring. Pin. Do this all the way around. Now begin lining up the drawn seam lines that you made earlier and place 2-3 pins between the pins that you have previously placed. Continue pinning all the way around.

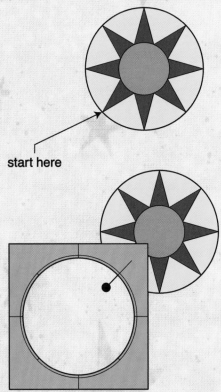

start here

- Sew on the drawn line, making sure to take out the pins as you come to them. Press.

• Make 4 corner sun units.

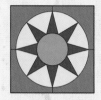

To assemble the quilt:

• Attach one **appliqué border strip** to each side of the quilt.

• Attach a **small sun unit** to each end of the remaining 2 borders.

• Attach **1 border to the top** and **1 to the bottom** of the quilt.

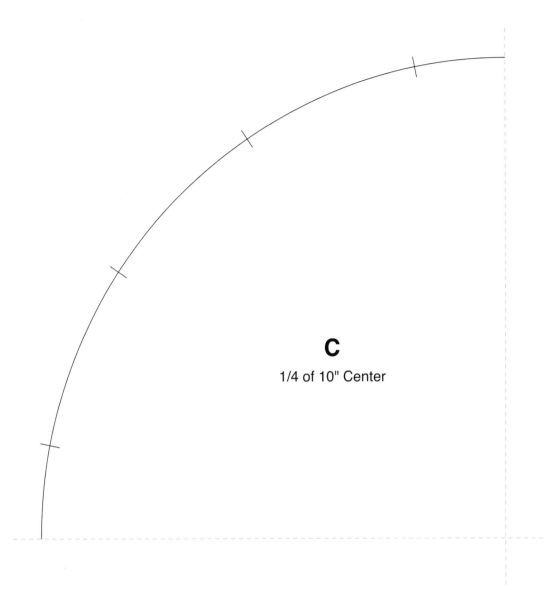

C

1/4 of 10" Center

To create pattern, make 4 copies of pattern piece C and tape together to make a 10" circle.

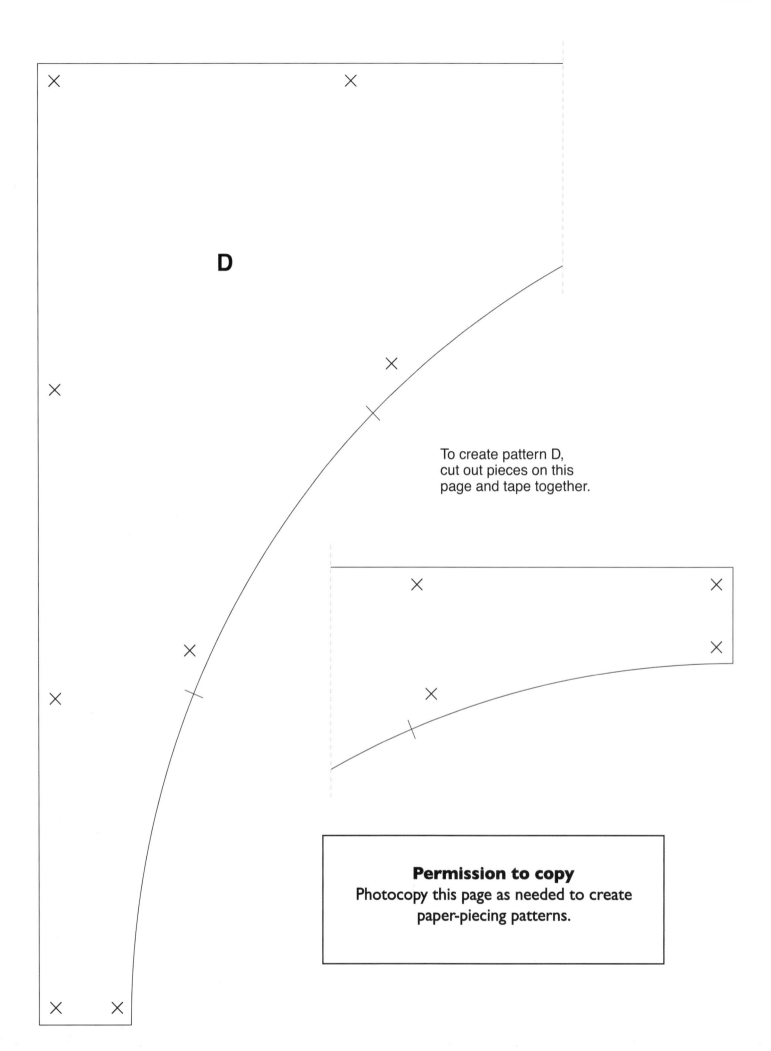

D

To create pattern D,
cut out pieces on this
page and tape together.

Permission to copy
Photocopy this page as needed to create
paper-piecing patterns.

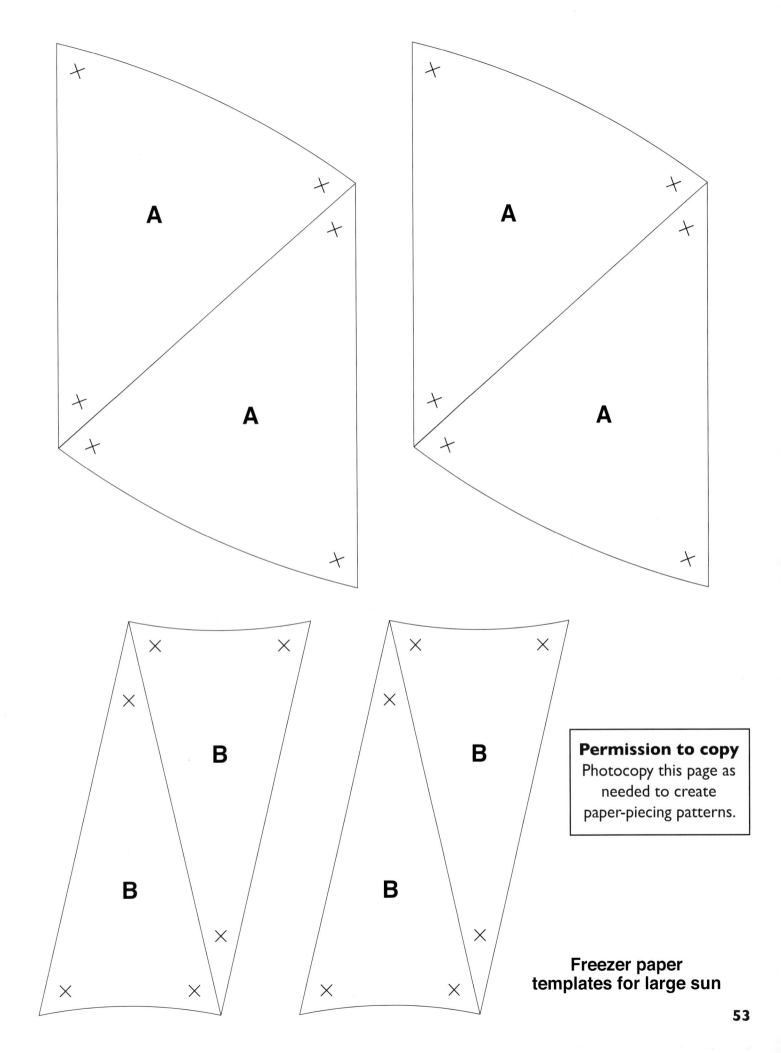

A

A

A

A

B

B

B

B

Freezer paper
templates for large sun

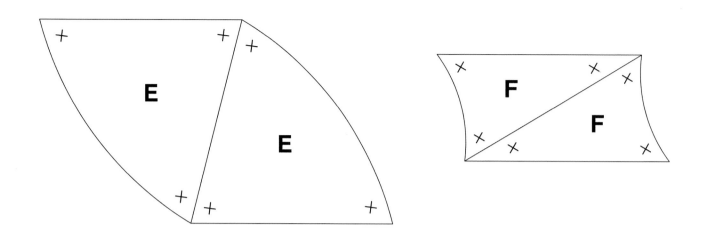

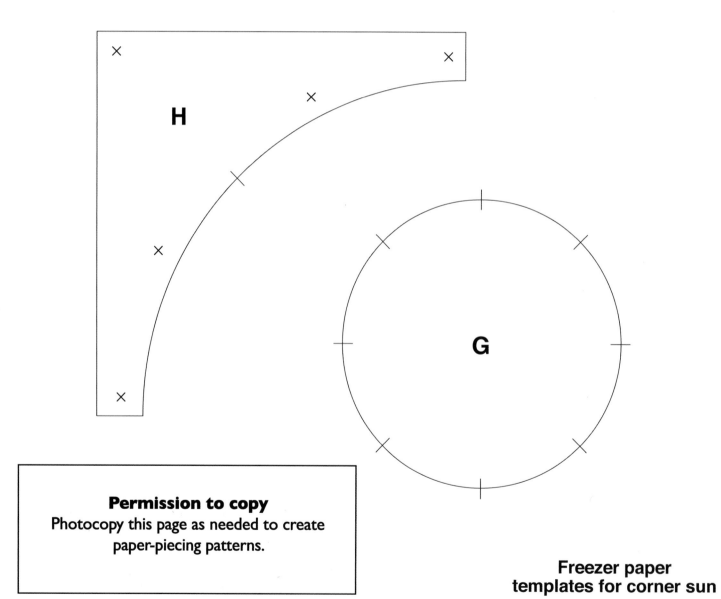

Freezer paper
templates for corner sun

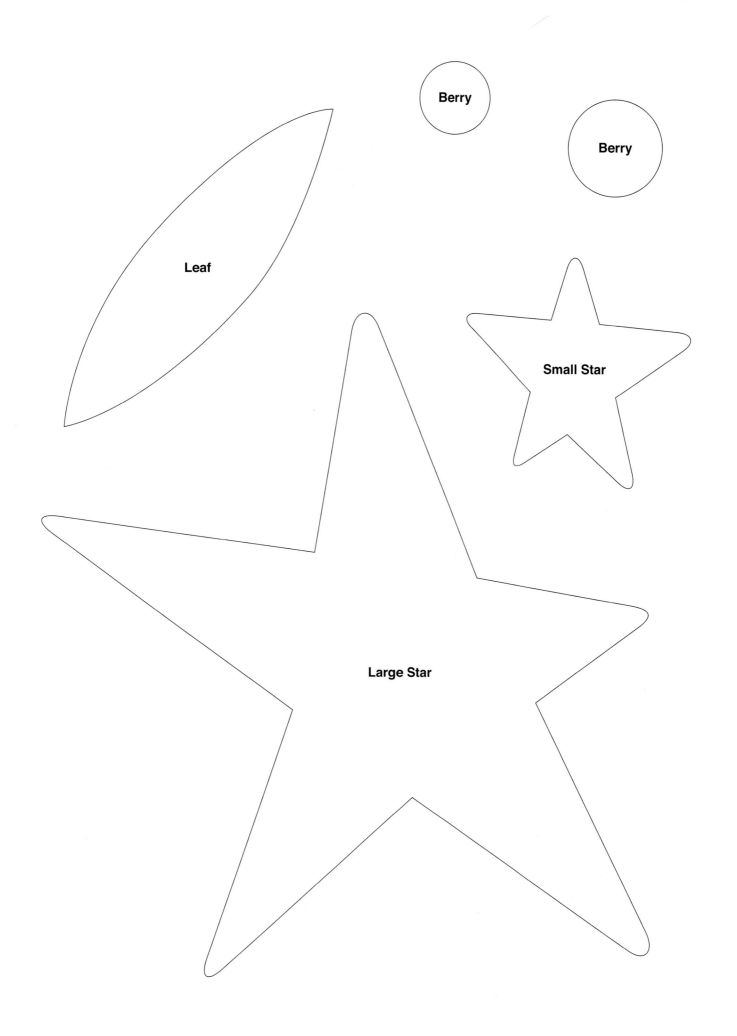

Berry

Berry

Leaf

Small Star

Large Star

STARRY NIGHT

CHAPTER 6

THE STARRY NIGHT

*For my part I know nothing with any certainty,
But the sight of the stars makes me dream.*

—Vincent Van Gogh

Vincent Van Gogh painted *The Starry Night* in 1889, in the final tortured days of his life. Unlike much of his work, he painted this piece from memory, not outdoors as was his preference.

Starry Night's roiling sky contains eleven stars. While Vincent didn't have the level of religious fervor in 1889 that he had experienced in his youth, there is speculation that the story of Joseph in the Old Testament may have had an influence on the painting's composition.

*'Look, I have had another dream' he said, 'I thought
I saw the sun, the moon and eleven stars, bowing
to me.'*

Genesis 37:9.

Today, *The Starry Night* is in the collection of The Museum of Modern Art in New York City.

Barbara Brackman
The stars and moon are featured in an imaginatively painted garage in Paxico, Kansas.

STARRY, STARRY NIGHT

Block size: 11 1/2"

Quilt size: 81" x 92"

Using the same flying geese technique used in the Evening Star block, you can piece this quilt accurately in a fairly short time. To balance the business of the pieced blocks, I used a beautiful large floral fabric for the border.

Fabric requirements:

- 30 fat eighths darks (red, gold, green and black)
- 15 fat eighths beiges
- 1/2 yard red
- 2 1/3 yards large floral

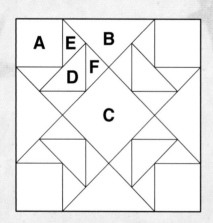

For each block cut:

- Cut 4 dark As – 3 3/8" x 3 3/8".

- Cut 1 dark B – 7" x 7". Cut in quarters diagonally.

- Cut 1 dark center C – 4 1/2" x 4 1/2".

- Cut 1 dark D – 5 1/4" x 5 1/4".

• Cut 4 light Es – 2 7/8" x 2 7/8".

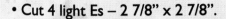

• Cut 4 light Fs – 2 7/8" x 2 7/8".
  Cut in half diagonally.

Assembling the block:

To make the flying geese unit:

• Draw diagonal lines on the **wrong** side of the 4 - 2 7/8" squares (E).

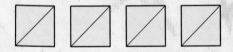

• Place 2 of these dark squares on **opposite corners** of the background square (D), right sides together, lining up drawn lines diagonally. Stitch 1/4" on each side of the drawn lines.

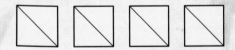

• Cut apart on the drawn line. Press open.

**** For added interest, switch the placement of light and dark fabric in the same blocks. This will give your quilt a more antique look.

• Place a light square on the corner of the large triangle, right sides together. Make sure the drawn diagonal line runs from the corner to the center. Stitch 1/4" on each side of the drawn line. Do this on both pieces.

• Cut apart on the drawn lines. Press open. Set aside.

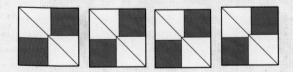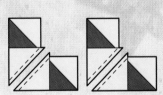

To make the corner geese unit:

- Sew one triangle F to one square A.

- Next attach another triangle F. Make 4 of these units.

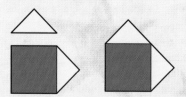

Final assembly:

Once you have the flying geese units and the corner geese units finished, it is time to assemble the block.

- **Make 4** of these combined units.

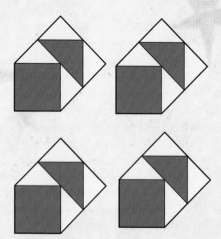

- Sew together as shown.

- You will need **30 blocks** for this quilt.

- Assemble the quilt **5 blocks wide** by **6 blocks long**, pinning carefully at the points.

Stop border:

- From the 1/2 yard of red fabric, cut 7 strips 2" x the width of the fabric. Trim off the selvedges. Sew these strips together to form one long strip.

- From this strip, cut **2 strips** 2" x 69 1/2". Attach 1 to each side of the quilt.

- Cut **2 more strip**s 2" x 61". Attach 1 to the top and 1 to the bottom of the quilt.

Final border:

- From the 2 1/3 yards of large floral, cut 2 strips 10 1/2" x 72 1/2". Attach 1 to each **side** of the quilt.

- Cut 2 more strips 10 1/2" x 81". Attach 1 to the **top** and 1 to the **bottom** of the quilt.

Watercolor of The Wizard of Oz's Glinda the Good Witch
by John C. Ralston

"...Kansas, she says, is the name of the star."
—Munchkins

LONESOME STAR

CHAPTER 7

ONE LONE STAR

The lone star was a popular theme for pioneers. Texas may be known as the lone star state, but early Kansas settlers used the star prominently when they created our state symbols.

The very bright John Ingalls, an orator, scholar, lawyer and statesman, coined the phrase "Ad astra per aspera" ("To the stars through difficulty") that became the Kansas state motto. He came to Kansas territory in 1859 to practice law, believing the state had a bright and promising future. He settled in Atchison and served as secretary of the state senate during the first legislative session following statehood.

Ingalls also designed a state seal. His seal was a single star rising from the clouds at the base of a field. At the top of the seal was a constellation of stars, representing the other states then in the Union. His rising star symbolized Kansas ascending to join the Union following a stormy struggle.

His original seal was modified, but his rising star remains a prominent part of today's Kansas state seal.

In his later years, Ingalls wrote for magazines and newspapers about the virtues of Kansas and his dreams for the state. He died in 1900 and was buried in Atchison.

Cherié Ralston
This star adorns a doorknob at the statehouse in Austin, Texas.

LONESOME STAR

Quilt size: 18 1/2" x 18 1/2"

Every year our quilt guild has a silent auction of mini quilts during our quilt show. The proceeds go to local charities. This will be my contribution this year. It is a fun, fast and interesting little quilt to make!

Fabric requirements:

- 1/3 yard dark blue
- 1/3 yard gold
- 2 fat eighths 2 different reds
- 3 fat eighths 3 different golds
- 1 fat eighth medium blue

Center block:

- From 1/3 yard dark blue, cut a **square** 10 1/2" x 10 1/2". Also, cut out and prepare the small star for appliqué.

- From 1/3 yard gold, cut out and prepare the **large star** for appliqué. Center the small blue star on the large gold star. Appliqué.

- **Center** the large gold star on the dark blue square. Appliqué.

Strip border:

- Cut **2 strips** 3/4" x 10 1/2". Attach 1 to each side of the center block.

- Cut **2 strips** 3/4" x 11". Attach 1 to the top and 1 to the bottom of the center block.

Sawtooth border:

- The sawteeth measure 1 1/2" finished. **Cut 5" squares** from each of the 4 gold fabrics, the 2 blues and the 2 reds. Pair 1 of each gold with 1 of each of the reds and blues. You can either use 1 1/2" finished Triangles on a Roll™, or you can cut a square 4 3/4" x 4 3/4". On the lighter fabric, **draw lines from corner to corner** on the diagonal in both directions.

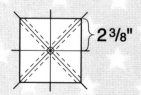

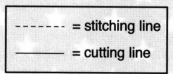

------- = stitching line

——— = cutting line

- Sew **1/4"** on each side of the drawn lines.

- Cut this square in **half** at 2 3/8" horizontally and vertically.

- **Cut** on your drawn diagonal lines. Press sawteeth open toward the dark fabric. This will yield 8 half square triangles for each of the 4 sets.

- Sew **2 strips** of 7 half square triangles without worrying about direction. **Do not press yet.*** Attach one to each side of the quilt. Press. (*Note: not pressing until now lets you ease in any extra fullness when attaching.)*

- Sew **2 strips of 9** half square triangles. **Do not press yet.*** Attach one to the top and one to the bottom. Press.

Appliqué border:

- From the 1/3 yard gold fabric, cut **2 strips** 3" x 14". Attach 1 to each side of the quilt. Press.

- Cut **2 strips** 3" x 19". Attach 1 to the top and 1 to the bottom of the quilt.

- From the dark blue, cut **6 bias strips** 3/4" wide. Pull strips through a #9 Clover™ bias tape maker (see source list at the back of the book) (or a 3/8" bias tape maker) to make 3/8" finished bias vine. Trim each vine to be **15" long.**

- Cut out and prepare **24 leaves** for appliqué. Baste vine and leaves in place, referring to the photo for placement. Appliqué.

Cherié Ralston
Stars hold together the Turnhalle, the turn-of-the-century beer garden on Rhode Island Street in Lawrence.

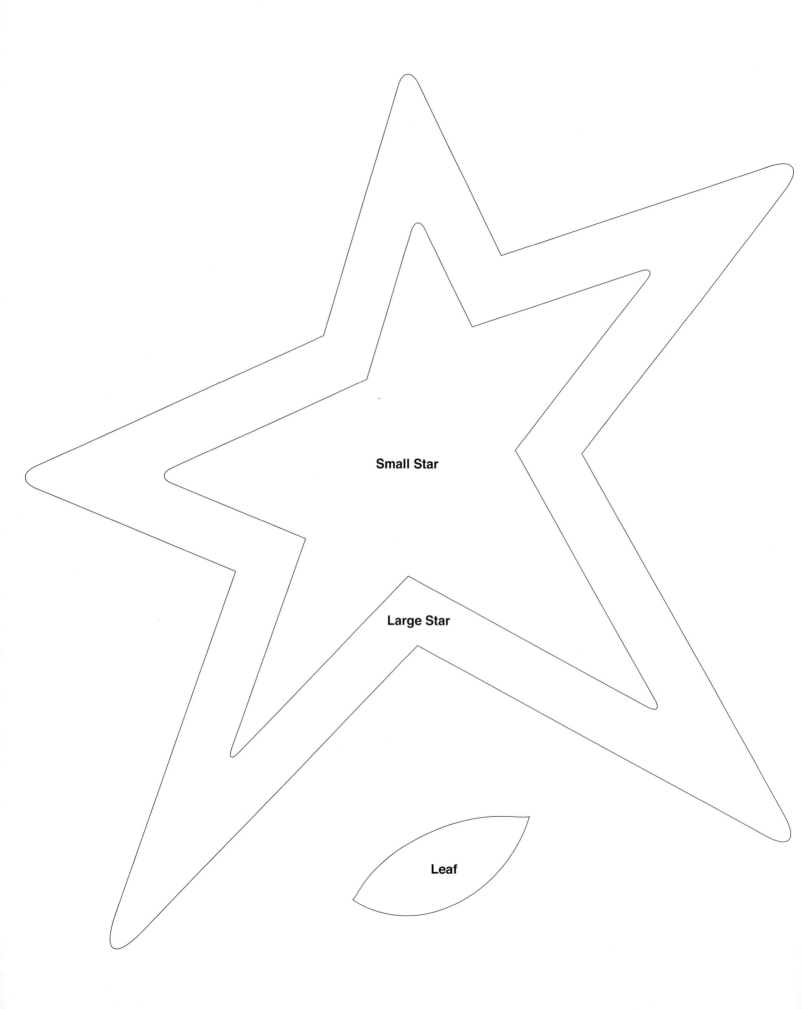

Small Star

Large Star

Leaf

CHAPTER 8

General instructions for punchneedle embroidery

Beware! Punchneedle is addictive! What a pleasure it is to draw a little picture on some fabric, put it in a hoop and with some colorful embroidery floss, transform your drawing into a lovely little work of folk art!

To do punchneedle, you need to purchase a punchneedle kit. Most include excellent instructions along with the needle. Refer to your booklet as you follow the instructions below.

Supplies needed:

• Igolochkoy™, CTR™, or comparable punchneedles for 1 and 3 strands

• Needle threader for punchneedle

• Embroidery floss

• 5" embroidery hoop with locking lip (or a hoop large enough to allow your design to be completely encompassed)

• Weavers cloth foundation fabric

• Small scissors

Threading the needle:

• The punchneedle is a hollow shaft with a sharp pointed end that has two different sides. One side is beveled (front): the eye of the needle lies within the bevel.

• **Thread the loop of the threader** with the desired number of strands of embroidery floss. When using more than one strand of floss, separate the strands and then put them back together. Doing this gives the thread more volume and makes it easier to work with.

• **Thread the point of the threader** into the base of the needle tool; pull the threader and thread out of the pointed end of the needle. Pull it out far enough to now pass the point of the threader through the eye of the needle – beveled side (front) toward the back.

• Remove the threader and **adjust the thread** so that about 1" is protruding from the tip of the needle. This keeps it from unthreading when you start punching.

Preparing a pattern

- **Trace** the desired pattern on the weavers cloth with a pencil or a fine pointed waterproof pen. Align the outside edge of the pattern with the straight grain of the fabric. A light table or a window is helpful for tracing.

Stitching:

- Place **the inner ring** of the hoop on the table with the locking lip up.

- Lay the **fabric over the ring** with the pattern side up. Open the nut on the outer ring and place it over the fabric; press down. Lift the rings slightly and continue to press the outer ring down over the lip. Tighten the nut to keep the hoops from falling apart. Work around the hoop, pulling the fabric taut and tightening the nut until your fabric is drum tight and the grain of the fabric has not distorted.

- With the drawing side up and your needle threaded with the correct number of strands, it's time to **start punching**. Hold the needle perpendicular to the fabric between your thumb and first two fingers with the thread coming out of the handle freely. Hold the handle like a pencil with the beveled side of the needle facing the direction you are punching. I punch toward myself, but you can punch in any direction as long as the beveled side of the needle leads.

- Begin punching just inside the pattern line. **Punch straight down** through the fabric until the gauge hits the fabric. Lift the needle back to the fabric surface, being careful not to lift the tip of the needle off the face of the fabric. Move a short distance scratching across the fabric; plunge the needle in again. Your stitches should be short enough so they make a continuous line of loops on the front with no spaces to be seen between stitches.

- When you want **to change directions**, leave your needle in and turn the needle or turn your hoop so the bevel faces the direction you want to move. Begin again by bringing the needle to the surface about a needle width away from the last row so you have a small amount of fabric showing between the rows.

- Continue in this manner until you are at the end of your thread or at a place where you want to stop. To stop before you are out of thread, **stop with the needle down**, place your finger on top of the last stitch and pull the needle up and away from the fabric. Clip this thread flush with the back. Also clip the ends of the thread where you started.

- Punch the **outline first**; then fill in the design. Finish by filling in the background.

- Turn your work over and **trim** any long threads flush with the loops.

How to frame your punchneedle work:

• Once the punching is done, **remove the piece** from the hoop.

• **Trim** away the excess weavers cloth, leaving 1 1/2" all the way around the design.

• **Zigzag or serge** the raw edges.

• Turn your frame over and **measure the inside** of the back of the frame.

• **Cut a piece of mat board** slightly smaller than this measurement. (The mat board should have a little wiggle room when placed in the frame.)

• Place your punchneedle on a table. **Center** the mat board over it.

• Draw the sides of the weavers cloth over the mat board and **tape** in place. Gently lift the piece and check to see if it is centered. Make adjustments as needed.

• Do the same for the top and bottom of the cloth.

• Once you are happy with the placement, remove the tape.

• With thread and needle, **lace the two sides together.**

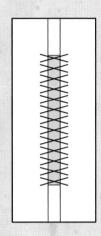

• Do the same for the **top and bottom.**

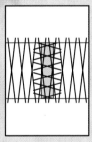

• Place your finished piece in the frame.

SUMMER GLORY PUNCHNEEDLE

SUMMER GLORY PUNCHNEEDLE

Supplies:

- 9" square weavers cloth
- 5" or 6" lip locking hoop
- 05 pigma pen
- 3-strand punchneedle tool
- 4" x 4" picture frame – Huneywood color # 553
  (available from Old Mill Stitchery - *see Sources at the end of the book*)

DMC embroidery floss used:

Flag pole – 3781
Star on flag – 729
Flag field – 3750
Red flag stripes – 221
White flag stripes – 739
Flowers – 2 strands 301, 1 strand 977
Buds – 301
Flower stems and leaves – 2 strands 732, 1 strand 733
Berries – 3740
Berry stems – 3011
Berry leaves – 2 strands 3011, 1 strand 732
Basket – 729
Star on basket – 3750
Background - 3 skeins 310
Gold outline border – 729

(Note: punchneedle is worked from the back of the canvas, so patterns are reversed for tracing purposes.)

STARLIGHT PUNCHNEEDLE

STARLIGHT PUNCHNEEDLE

Supplies:

• 9" square weavers cloth
• 5" or 6" lip locking hoop
• 05 pigma pen
• 1-strand punchneedle tool
• 3-strand punchneedle tool
• 3" x 3" picture frame

DMC embroidery floss used:

Moon – 926
Stars – 3033 – (1 strand only)
Leaves – 2 strands 731, 1 strand 734
Tree trunk – 2 strands 829, 1 strand 612
Background – 2 strands 3777, 1 strand 918
Border – 310

SHELTERING TREE PUNCHNEEDLE

SHELTERING TREE PUNCHNEEDLE

Supplies:

- 9" square weavers cloth
- 5" or 6" lip locking hoop
- 05 pigma pen
- 3-strand punchneedle tool
- 2" x 3" picture frame

DMC embroidery floss used:

Tree trunk – 2 threads 611, 1 thread 931
Windows and door - 310
Bird body -926
Bird wing - 3768
Star - 422
Roof and house edge – 3799
Leaves – 2 threads 730, 1 thread 733
House - 3777
Fence - 801
Grass - 733
Chimney - 301

Gentle Art Simply Shaker embroidery floss used:

Butternut Squash—3 skeins

HARVEST MOON PUNCHNEEDLE

HARVEST MOON PUNCHNEEDLE

Supplies:

• 9" square weavers cloth
• 5" or 6" lip locking hoop
• .05 pigma pen
• 3-strand punchneedle tool
• 2" x 3" picture frame

DMC embroidery floss:

White pumpkin outline – 370
Orange pumpkin fill – 436
Moon – 3777
Stars – 523
Bird body - 729
Bird wing – 3045
Bird legs and pumpkin stems – 829
Berries - 3740
Leaf outline, stems and vines – 732
Background and bird eye – 310
Line border - 436

Weeks Dye Works floss used:

White pumpkin fill – Light Khaki
Orange pumpkin outline – Cognac
Bird eye and background – 3 skeins Mascara
Sampler Threads floss used:
Leaf fill – Cornhusk
(see source list at back of book)

CATCH A FALLING STAR RUG/FOOTSTOOL

CHAPTER 9

CATCH A FALLING STAR RUG/FOOTSTOOL

These instructions are to make a finished rug, but I used this design to hook a cover for a footstool I found at an antique store. Look around at antique shops for a footstool that can be covered with a hooked piece. Adapt the design to fit your find!

Fabric requirements:

- 6 different red wools - 14" x 18" each
- Cheddar wool - 4" x 12"
- 3 yellow wools - 3" x 12" each
- 3 different green wools - 10" x 18" each
- Black wool (we used overdyed antique black) – 30" x 18"
- Choose different textures of wool... plaids, hand dyed and "as is" wool will add depth to your project.

Supplies:

- Monks cloth
- Red dot tracer (transparent fiber cloth printed with a grid of red dots at 1" intervals)
- Black Sharpie® marking pen
- Wool cutter with #5 (5/32") and #7 (7/32") blade
- Wool yarn for binding
- 2 yards 1 1/4" twill tape for binding

Directions:

- **Trace the pattern** onto the red dot tracer with the black Sharpie® marking pen.

- Mark the outermost border of your rug on the monks cloth, making sure to stay on the straight of grain.

- Place the red dot tracing on top of the monks cloth. With the pen, draw over the drawing to **transfer it** to the fabric.

- Use the #5 blade (5/32") on your cutter to cut the wool for the tree, stars, berries and leaves.

- Use the #7 blade (7/32") on your cutter to cut the wool for the background and border.

- Once you are ready to start, **hook** the tree, stars, leaves and berries. Last, hook the background and the border.

- Place your finished rug face down on a **dampened towel.** Press with a steam iron on medium/high. Let dry. Flip it over and repeat.

- **Trim** the excess monks cloth to 1 1/4". Zigzag the raw edge of the monks cloth. With a heavy thread or yarn, sew a running stitch 1/2" from the zigzag edge.

- **Bind the edge** with wool yarn to match or contrast with your rug. I use 1 strand of worsted-weight washed wool yarn. Fold the monks cloth to the back of the rug, leaving 1/4" showing and mitering the corners. To miter, fold the corners in first, then fold in the 4 sides. Pin in place.

- With a Clover™ Jumbo Tapestry Needle with a bent point, bury **2" of the end** of a 24" length of wool in the fold, exiting near the front edge loops of your rug. Throw the thread over the fold and take a stitch from the back of the rug, through the monks cloth. Exit right next to where you first exited.

- **Continue to sew** over the fold with very close stitches. When you are at the end of your yarn, bury this end between the fold and the stitches you just made.

- To start again with a new length of thread, bury the end as before and begin stitching where your last stitch ended.

- You will have **to take extra stitches** on the corners making sure none of the monks cloth shows through the yarn. Continue in this manner until the whole rug is bound.

- **Cover the raw edge** of the monks cloth on the back of the rug with 1 1/4" wide twill tape, mitering the corners. Whip stitch down both edges all the way around.

Star Rug/Footstool Pattern-25%
(To create full size pattern, cut out pattern sections on the following 3 pages and tape together as shown above.)

CHAPTER 10

DIVINE STAR VINE TOTE

I am always on the lookout for the perfect tote. It has to be big enough to carry a project to my weekly sewing group, but not so big that things get lost in the bottom. A front pocket is handy and the straps have to be just the right length to slip over your shoulder. I think this tote has it all. You could easily make several for your quilting friends!

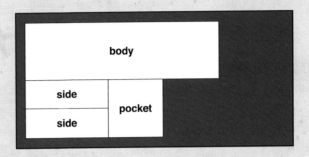

Supplies:

- 5/8 yard red Sandcastle – or any heavyweight fabric
- 2 yards cotton webbing 1" wide
- 3" x 12" black wool
- scraps of gold, black and red wool
- 3" x 10" green wool

Cutting:

- Cut 1 rectangle 12" x 36" for **tote body**.

- Cut 2 rectangles 6" x 15" for **tote sides.**

- Cut 1 square 12" x 12" for **pocket** (you can cut 2 pockets if you wish).

- **Zigzag** stitch or serge all cut edges of the rectangles and square to prevent fraying.

Pocket:

- Fold one end of the 12" square over 1/4" and topstitch. This will be the **bottom of the pocket.**

- Fold the opposite end over 1" and topstitch. This will be the **top of the pocket.** Set aside.

Wool band:

- From the 3" x 10" green wool, cut or tear a strip 1/2" x 10" for the **vine**. Cut out 3 leaves.

- Cut the **star flower** from the gold wool.

- Cut the **star center** from the scrap of black.

- Cut **4 small berries**.

- Referring to the photo for placement, **arrange the shapes**. Whip stitch all in place.

- Place this strip **1" down** from the top edge of the pocket.

- **Topstitch** approximately 1/8" from the edge on each side.

- **Measure** down 4" from the top edge of the tote body. Place the top of the pocket there. Pin the sides and bottom in place. Sew a double line of topstitching at the bottom of the pocket.

- Sew a **basting stitch** on each side of the pocket 1/4" from the edge to hold it in place.

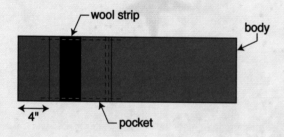

wool strip

body

4"

pocket

Construction:

- Place the large rectangle on your ironing board, with the right side up. Measure 12" from the top and bottom edge. Place a **pin in this spot** on each side of the large rectangle.

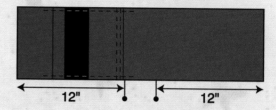

12"   12"

side rectangle   **Fig. 1**

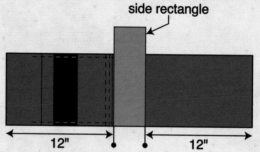

12"   12"

- Place one of the **side rectangles** as shown in Fig. 1, right sides together. Stitch with a 1/4" seam allowance, starting 1/4" from the edge, and ending 1/4" from the other edge. Backstitch at beginning and end. (see Fig. 2)

- Repeat the step above to **add the other side.** You have just attached the sides to the bottom of the tote.

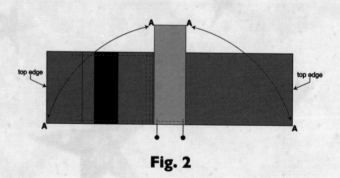

top edge   top edge

Fig. 2

- Now **match up point A** on the side rectangle with point A at the top of the body of the tote. Pin along the edge. Sew with 1/4" seam allowance from top to bottom stopping at the same point as the bottom of the tote. Repeat for the other side. You now have a tote without handles.

Attaching the handles:

• Cut 2 pieces of webbing 28" long.

• With bag **inside out,** fold the top edge down 1/2". Press and topstitch.

• **Fold** the same edge down again 1" and press.

• Measure in 3" from the edge of the bag where the side panel is attached. (Fig. 3)

• **Pin the web handles in place,** as shown, between the pins, slipping the ends under the 1" seam allowance. Do this on both sides.

• **Topstitch** along both edges. Remove pins.

• Fold the handles up (Fig. 3) and **stitch ends securely** with a square and X as shown in Figs. 4 and 5.

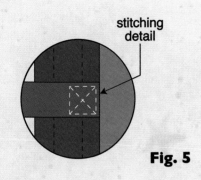

Fig. 5

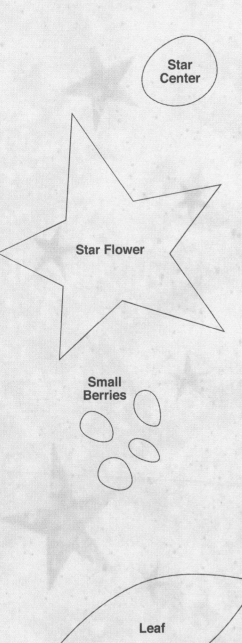

Star Center

Star Flower

Small Berries

Leaf

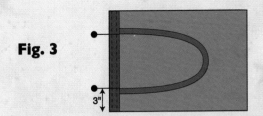

Fig. 3

3"

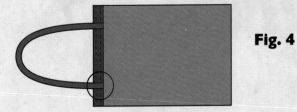

Fig. 4

CHAPTER 11

AMY'S SEWING KIT

Fill this tote with your punchneedle tools or your favorite quilting tools!

Supplies:

- Timeless Tote™ zippered accessory tote – 9" x 12"
- 24 1/2" x 10" pumpkin wool
- 24 1/2" x 10" fabric for lining
- 6" x 9" dark teal wool
- 4" x 9" gold wool
- 2" x 2" light teal wool
- HeatnBond™ Ultra Hold
- #5 perle cotton – Mascara and Amber – Weeks Dye Works (see source list at the back of the book)

To make the cover of your tote:

- Layer the pumpkin colored wool and the cotton fabric right sides together. Pin well, as the wool will shift a bit. With the wool on the bottom, **sew** a 1/4" seam around the perimeter, leaving a 4" space on the side for turning. Trim corners, turn and press, making sure the edges and corners are neat. Whip stitch the opening closed. **Remove** the hook side of the Velcro™ that comes on the tote to use on the cover. Measure down 1" from the top of the cover and center the loop side of the Velcro™.

Sew in place. This will now be the **back** of the closed tote.

- **Trace** the tree, bird and small star onto HeatnBond™ Ultra Hold, leaving approximately 1/2" between shapes. *The templates provided have been reversed for use with Heat-nBond.* Cut them apart, leaving approximately 1/4" between shapes.

- **Iron** the tree onto the dark teal wool, the bird onto the gold wool, and the star onto the light teal wool. Be sure to follow the manufacturer's directions. It only takes a few seconds for the bond to work.

- Carefully **cut out each shape** on the lines. Remove the paper backing from the wool shapes.

- **Position the tree, bird and light teal star** onto the front of the wool cover. Iron in place, whip stitch down.

- Use the Amber perle cotton to **quilt around the tree, bird and small star.** Quilt your initials next to the tree.

- With the Mascara perle cotton, make a **french knot** for the bird's eye. **Quilt** around the entire perimeter of the cover about 1/4" from the edge. Stem stitch the thread from the bird's mouth to the star.

- Open the Timeless Tote™ (Fig. 1) and **position the finished cover** on top of it as shown in the drawing. The Velcro™ closure will now be on the back of the tote as to not interfere with the design on the front. Pin in place along the very edge. If the cover has stretched a bit during stitching, just ease the excess into place. Wool is very forgiving as you work.

- **Whip stitch** the cover to the tote all the way around making sure that when you come to the web handles and strap, you stitch all the way through them into the edge of the tote.

Cherié Ralston

Even from the Pennsylvania Street alley, stars peek out from this house.

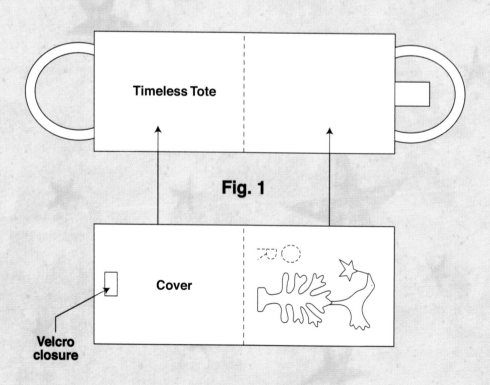

Fig. 1

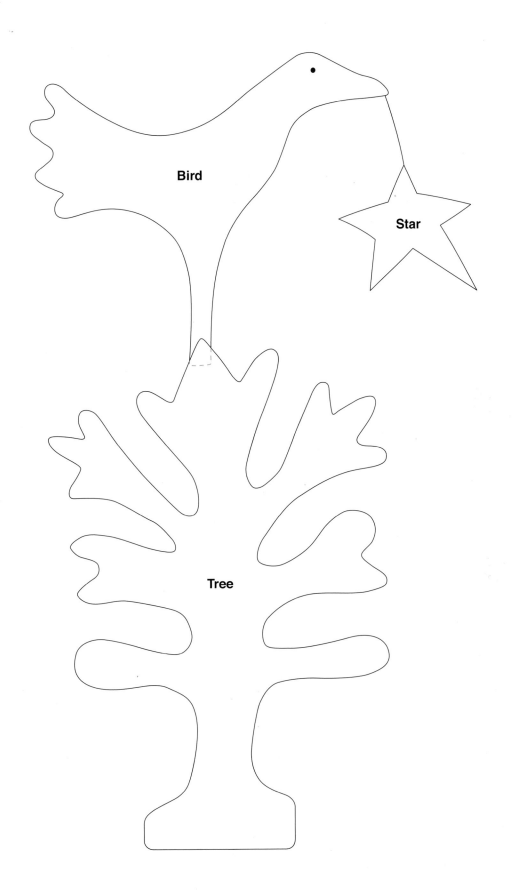

Bird

Star

Tree

CHAPTER 12

HOOKED CHAIR PAD

All chair pads that follow were designed to be hooked or made in penny rug style. They can also be used as fun little placemats! If you can take a rug hooking class at your local quilt shop, you should do so. Your teacher can share her knowledge and will give you a good background in hooking.

Fabric requirements:

• 3 red wools totaling 12" x 16"
• Purple wool 7" x 13"
• 4 gold wools totaling 14" x 16"
• light green wool 4" x 17"
• 2 blue wools totaling 40" x 16"

Supplies:

• Monks cloth
• Red dot tracer for tracing and transferring the design. See instructions below.
• Black Sharpie® marking pen
• Wool yarn for binding
• 1 1/4" Twill tape for binding
• Wool cutter with a #7 blade

Directions:

• **Trace** the pattern onto the red dot tracer.

• Place the red dot tracing on top of the monks cloth. With a Sharpie® pen, trace over the drawing to **transfer** it to the fabric.

• **Cut the wool strips** with a #7 blade on your cutter or cut strips 7/32" with your rotary cutter and mat.

• **Hook** the stars, vines and berries. Lastly, hook the background and the border.

• Place your finished chair pad face down on a dampened towel. **Press** with a steam iron on medium/high. Let dry. Flip it over and repeat.

• **Trim** the excess monks cloth to 1 1/4". Zigzag the raw edge of the monks cloth.

With a heavy thread or yarn, sew a running stitch 1/2" from the zigzag edge. Gently pull on the yarn to ease in the excess monks cloth.

• **Bind the edge** with wool yarn. *(see instructions with the Chapter 9 rug/footstool)*

• **Cover the raw edge** on the back of the mat with 1 1/4" wide twill tape. This is a little tricky. You can use the same gathering method you used on the monks cloth to ease in the excess twill tape.

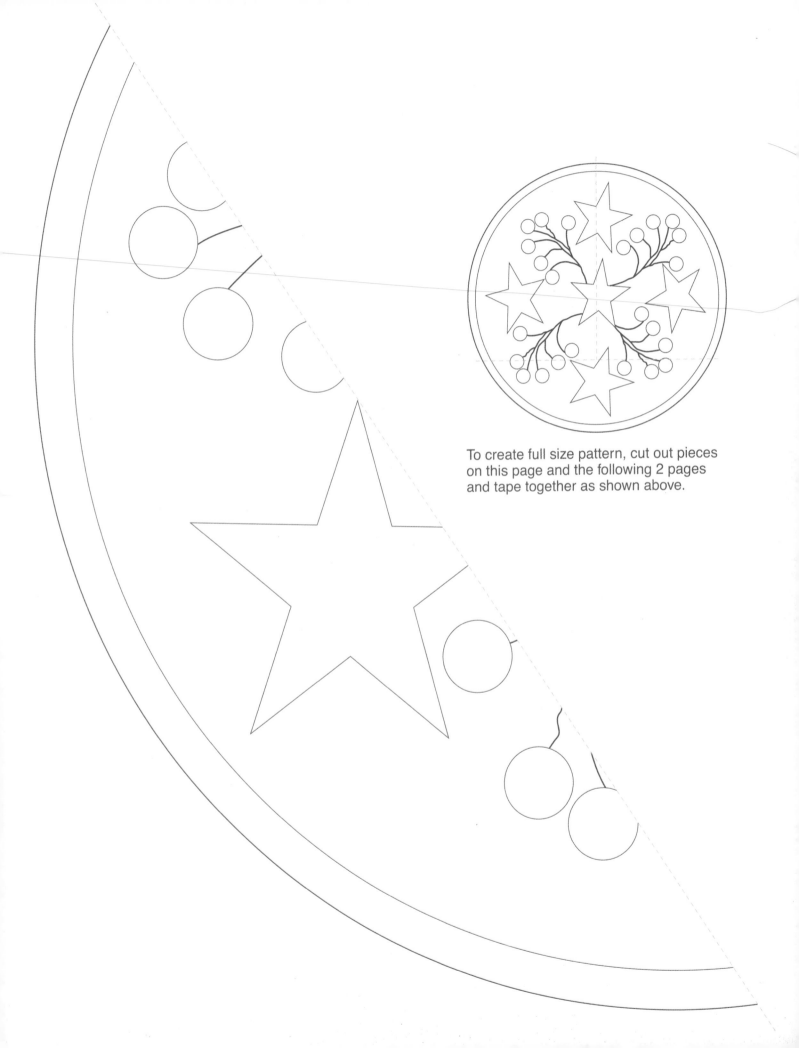

To create full size pattern, cut out pieces on this page and the following 2 pages and tape together as shown above.

PENNY RUG CHAIR PADS

These penny rugs are so much fun to make—and fast too. Instructions follow for making them in wool, but these designs would easily adapt to become rugs or quilts. I've been using mine for placemats instead of chair pads.

Fabric requirements for Star Wreath:

- 15" square black wool
- 11" x 15" hand-dyed gold wool
- 13" square blue wool
- 3" square purple
- 7" x 9" hand-dyed green
- 1/2 yard green plaid
- #5 Perle cotton - black
- HeatnBond™ lite

Directions:

- **Trace** the large circle (14") onto a piece of freezer paper. This will help stabilize the wool when you cut it out. Cut out the paper, leaving 1/8" beyond the drawn line.

- **Iron** this onto the black wool. Cut out smoothly on the drawn line. Remove paper.

- **Trace** the medium circle, the large star, the small circle, and the small star, leaving about 1/2" between motifs, onto the HeatnBond. Trace the **25 leaves** onto the HeatnBond. These can be positioned very close together.

- Bond the **medium and small circles** onto the gold wool. Cut out smoothly on the drawn lines.

- Bond the **large star** onto the blue wool. Cut out smoothly on the drawn line.

- Bond the **small star** onto the purple wool. Cut out smoothly on the drawn line.

- Bond the **leaves** as one sheet onto the green wool. Cut out smoothly on the drawn lines. Remove paper.

- Remove the paper from the purple star, center it on the small gold circle. **Press to bond**, following the manufacturer's instructions. Remove the paper from the small circle. Appliqué.

To appliqué in place, use a machine embroidery **thread that matches** the color you are appliquéing. You can whip stitch by hand or appliqué by machine. When stitching by machine, I use the same stitch that I use for invisible machine appliqué with a bigger width and length.

(see Invisible Machine Appliqué instructions on page 127.) **You can also use a small zigzag stitch.**

- **Position the small gold circle** with the purple star in the center of the large blue star. Bond. Remove the paper from the **large blue star** and appliqué the circle. Set aside.

- Remove the paper from the **large gold circle**. Center the circle on the black background. Iron to bond. Appliqué.

- Center the **large star** on top of the gold circle. Appliqué.

- Place the **leaves** around the gold circle and appliqué as show in the drawing.

Backing:

- **Cut 2 -15 1/2"** green plaid circles. Place right sides together. Stitch with a 1/4" seam allowance all the way around, leaving a 3" opening for turning.

- **Turn right side out.** Whip stitch the opening closed. Press so edges are smooth and neat.

- Center the wool piece on top of the plaid circle. Pin in place. Using perle cotton, **hand stitch** around the circumference of the black wool with a blanket stitch.

To create full size pattern, cut out pieces on this page and the following 2 pages and tape together as shown above.

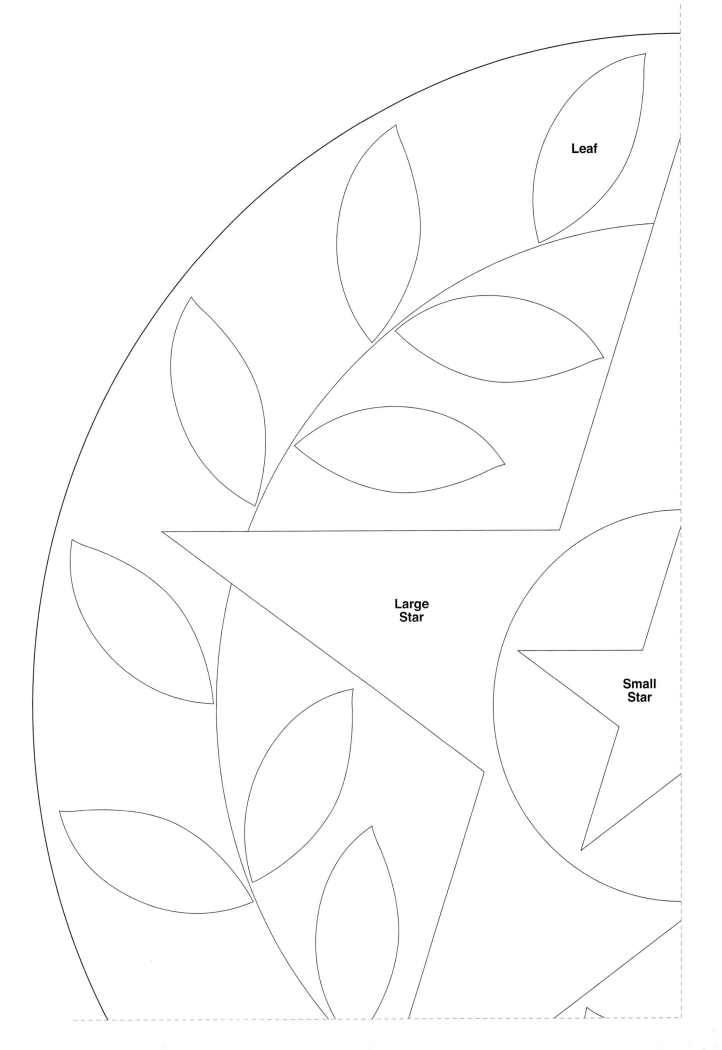

Leaf

Large
Star

Small
Star

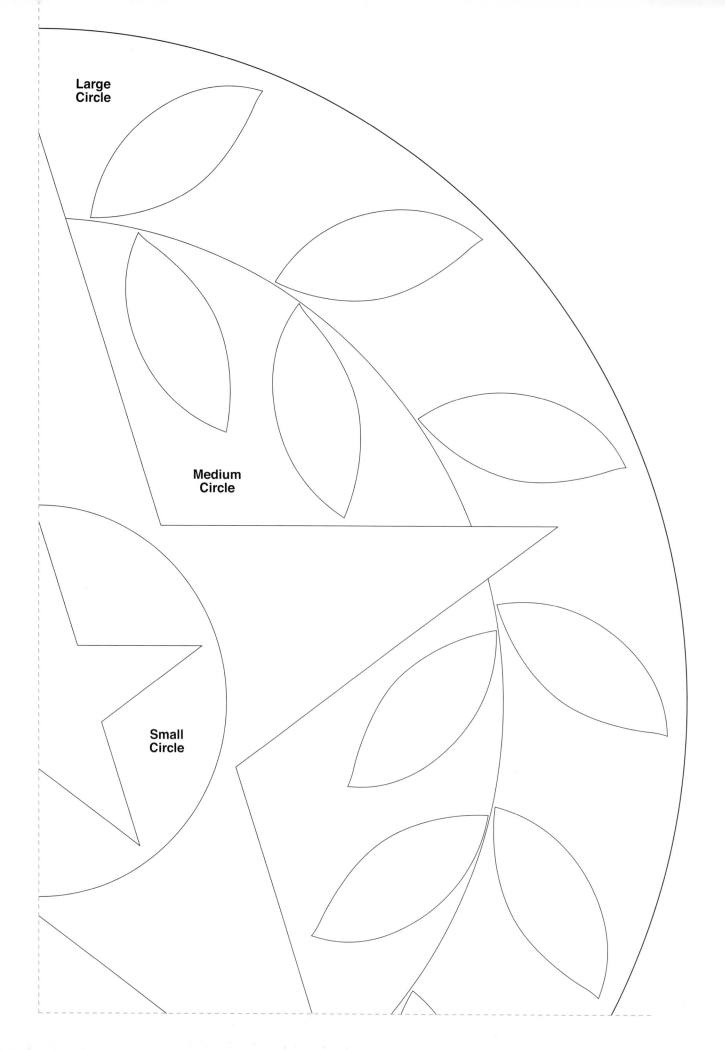

Large
Circle

Medium
Circle

Small
Circle

DESERT STAR

Fabric requirements:

- 10" x 15" rectangle black wool
- 15" square red plaid wool
- 7" square yellow/green wool
- 1/2 yard green plaid
- #5 perle cotton - black
- HeatnBond™ lite

Directions:

- **Trace** the large circle (14") onto a piece of freezer paper. This will help stabilize the wool when you cut it out. Cut out the paper, leaving 1/8" beyond the drawn line.

- Iron this onto the **black wool**. Cut out smoothly on the drawn line. Remove paper.

- Trace the **sawtooth circle** onto the HeatnBond™. Roughly cut out the sawtooth circle.

- Trace the large, medium and small stars on the HeatnBond™. Cut out roughly, leaving approximately 1/8" all the way around.

- **Bond** the sawtooth circle to the red plaid wool. Cut out the sawtooth circle smoothly on the drawn lines. Remove the paper.

- Center the **sawtooth circle** and fuse it to the black wool. Appliqué.

- Bond the **large and small stars** to the 10" x 15" piece of black wool. Cut out on the drawn lines. Set aside.

- Bond the **medium star** to the yellow/green wool. Cut out on the drawn line.

- Remove the paper and **center** the small black star inside the medium yellow/green star. Fuse. Remove the paper from the yellow/green star and appliqué.

- Center the **yellow/green star on the large black star**. Fuse. Remove the paper from the large black star. Appliqué.

- Center the **black star** on the sawtooth circle. Fuse and appliqué.

Backing:

- **Cut 2 -15 1/2"** green plaid circles. Place right sides together. Stitch with a 1/4" seam allowance all the way around, leaving a 3" opening for turning.

- **Turn right side out.** Whip stitch the opening closed. Press so edges are smooth and neat.

- **Center** the wool piece on top of the plaid circle. Pin in place. Using perle cotton, hand stitch around the circumference of the black wool with a blanket stitch.

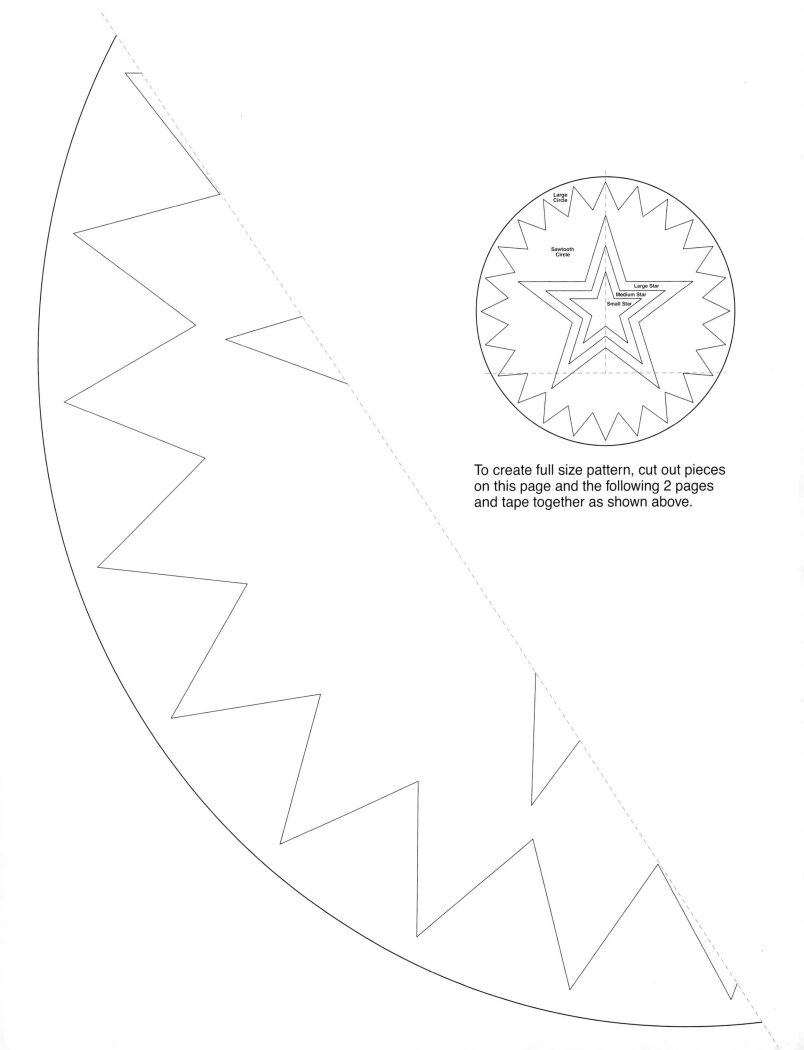

To create full size pattern, cut out pieces
on this page and the following 2 pages
and tape together as shown above.

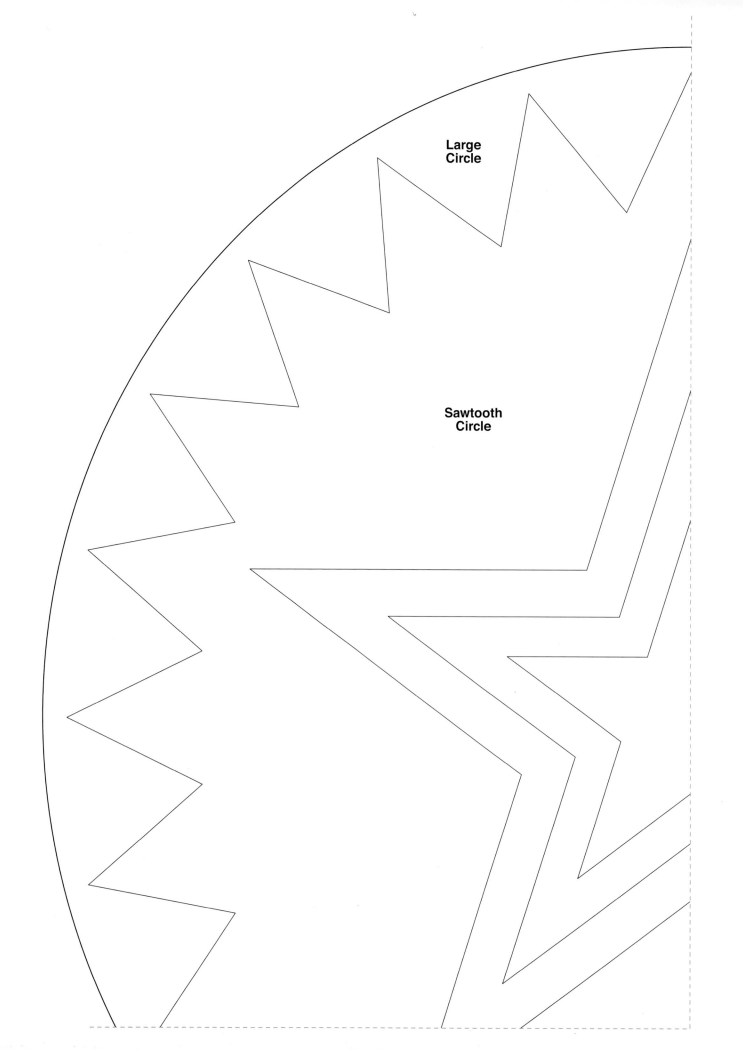

Large
Circle

Sawtooth
Circle

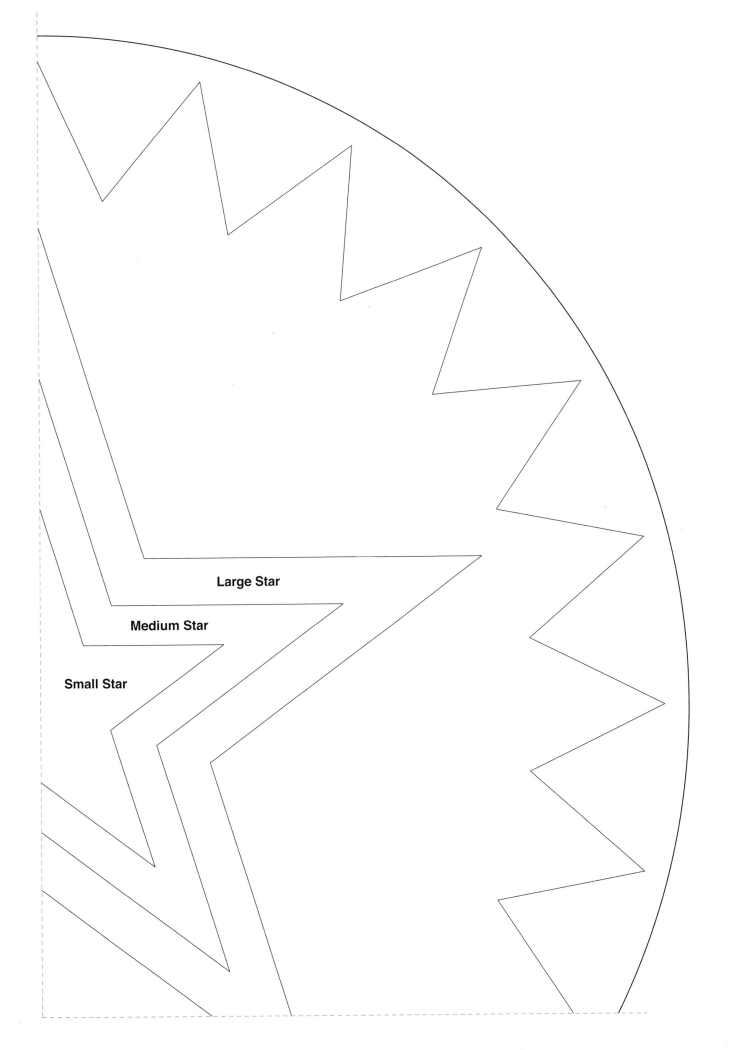

Large Star

Medium Star

Small Star

COWBOY STAR

Fabric requirements:

- 15" square black wool
- 13" square gold plaid wool
- 10" square red plaid wool
- 1/2 yard green plaid
- #5 perle cotton - black
- HeatnBond™ lite

Directions:

- **Trace** the large circle (14") onto a piece of freezer paper. This will help stabilize the wool when you cut it out. Cut out the paper, leaving 1/8" beyond the drawn line.

- Iron this onto the **black wool**. Cut out smoothly on the drawn line. Remove paper.

- **Trace** inner ring, the star, and the medium circle onto the HeatnBond. Trace the **25**

small circles very closely together. Roughly cut out the ring, the medium circle and the star, leaving approximately 1/8 around each motif. Leave the 25 small circles together on one piece.

- Bond the HeatnBond **inner ring** to the gold wool. Cut out smoothly on the drawn lines. Set aside.

- Bond the sheet of **25 small circles and the medium circle** to the black wool. Cut out smoothly on the drawn lines. Remove the paper. Space the small circles evenly around the ring. Bond, remove the paper from the ring, and appliqué.

- Bond the **star** to the red wool. Cut out smoothly on the drawn lines.

- Bond the **medium circle** to the center of the star. Remove the paper from the star and appliqué. Center the star with the ring over the points of the star on the black wool background. Press to bond. Appliqué the outer ring and the inner ring. Appliqué the star.

Backing:

- **Cut 2 -15 1/2"** green plaid circles. Place right sides together. Stitch with a 1/4" seam allowance all the way around, leaving a 3" opening for turning.

- **Turn right side out.** Whip stitch the opening closed. Press so edges are smooth and neat.

- **Center** the wool piece on top of the plaid circle. Pin in place. Using perle cotton, hand stitch around the circumference of the black wool with a blanket stitch.

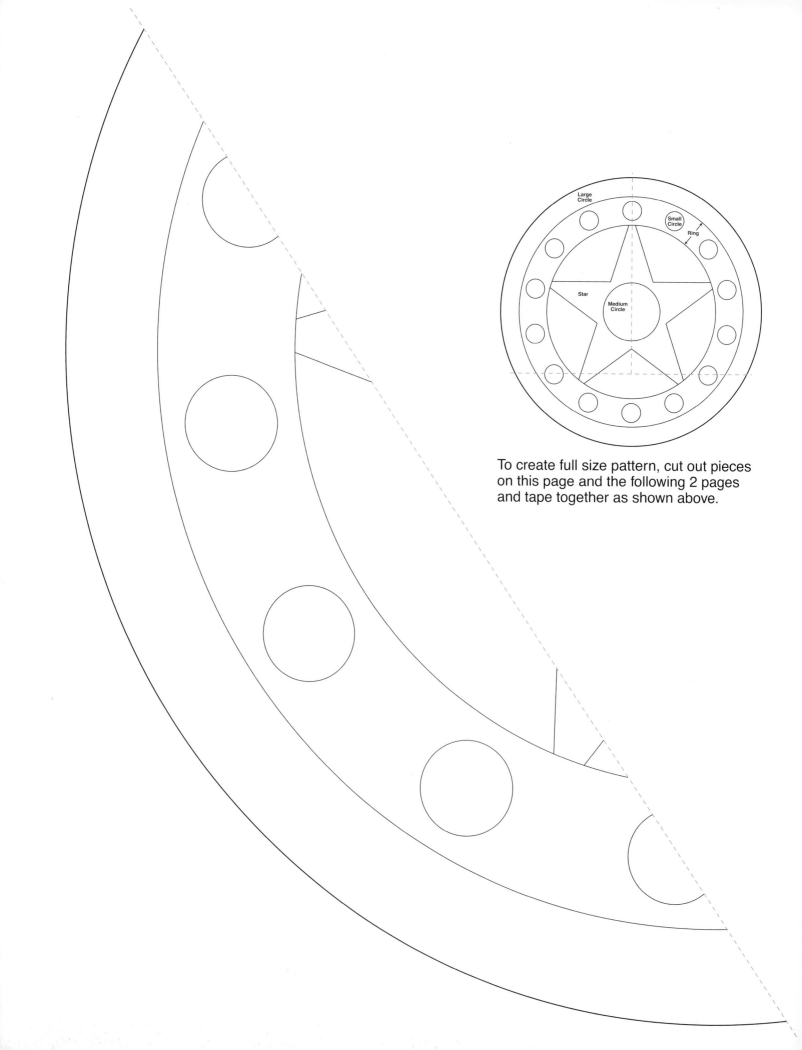

To create full size pattern, cut out pieces on this page and the following 2 pages and tape together as shown above.

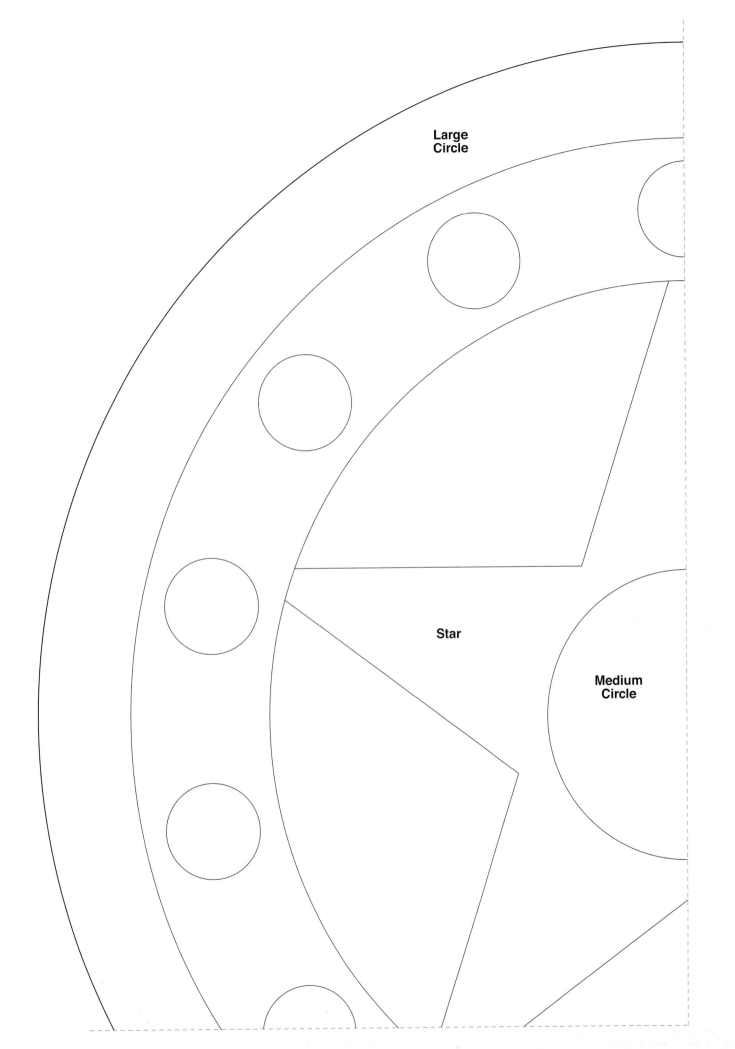

Large
Circle

Star

Medium
Circle

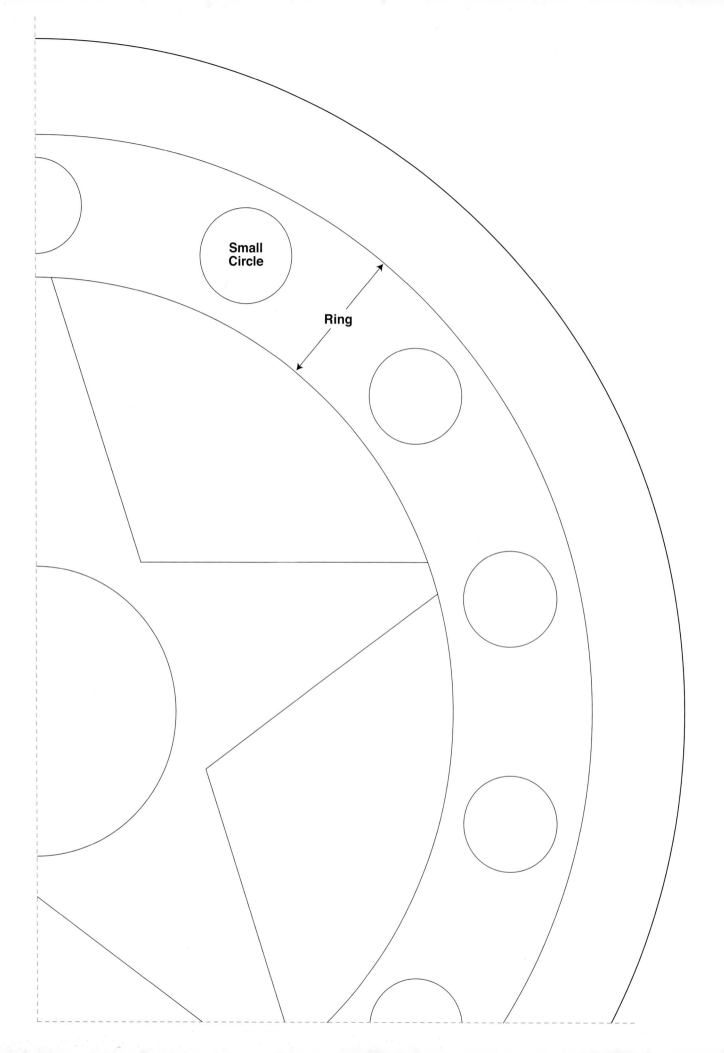

Small
Circle

Ring

DANCING STAR DATE BOOK

CHAPTER 13

DANCING STAR DATE BOOK

I love to make book covers! Each one can be different and colorful and if you get tired of one, you can make another to replace it. See the lessons in the back of the book for my formula to cover practically any book. Have fun and be creative with designs of your own!

Fabric requirements:

• Fat quarter brick colored wool
• 4" x 5" light green wool
• 5" x 5" dark green plaid wool
• 3" x 3" butter yellow wool
• 10" x 16" black wool

Supplies:

• Wavy rotary cutter blade or pinking shears
• DayMinder® G400-00 (available at office supply stores)
• Black perle cotton #8

Directions:

• From the brick colored wool, cut 1 rectangle 9 3/4" x 15 3/4".

• From the black wool, cut 2 rectangles 9 3/4" x 7 1/4".

• On a piece of HeatnBond™ lite, trace the **large star**, the **small star** and **5 leaves**, leaving about 1/4" between motifs. Roughly cut apart the stars, leaving at least 1/8" all around the drawn line. Keep the leaves together in one piece.

• Following the manufacturer's instructions, bond the **large star** onto the dark green plaid wool. Carefully cut out on the drawn line.

• Bond the **small star** onto the butter yellow wool. Carefully cut out on the drawn line. Remove the paper backing.

• Center the **small star** on the **large star.** Bond. Remove the paper from the large star and appliqué the small star.

To appliqué in place, use a machine embroidery thread that matches the color you are appliquéing. You can whip stitch by hand or appliqué by machine. When stitching by machine, I use the same stitch that I use for invisible machine appliqué with a bigger width and length (see *Invisible Machine Appliqué instructions on page 127.*) You can also use a small **zigzag** stitch.

- Bond the sheet of **leaves** onto the light green wool. Carefully cut out on the drawn lines. Remove the paper backing.

- Position the **small star/large star unit** and the leaves in place on the right hand side of the brick wool cover. Fold the cover in half to make sure you will be happy with the placement. Bond and appliqué.

- Place the book cover **wrong side up**. Place the 2 black rectangles on top of this to form your book cover. Pin well.

- Using perle cotton, **stitch 1/4"** from the edge with a large quilting stitch all the way around the edge of the book.

- Slip your calendar inside.

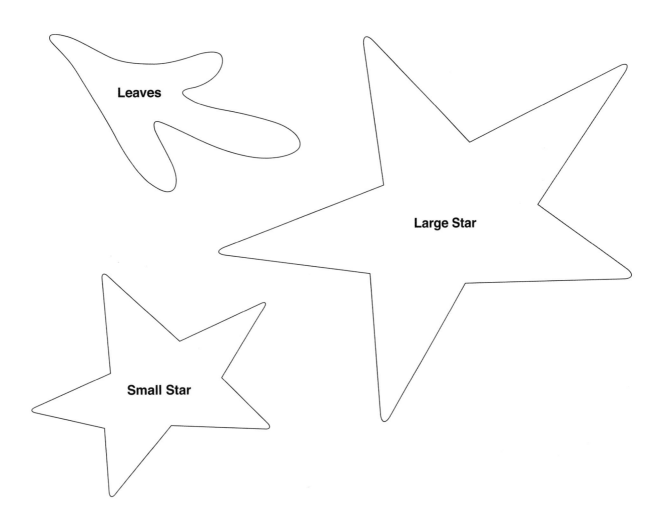

Leaves

Large Star

Small Star

STARFLOWER POCKET CALENDAR

CHAPTER 14

STARFLOWER POCKET CALENDAR

One Christmas, I made eight of these date book covers (all with different, personalized motifs) for each of the women in my quilt group. They are fun to make and make wonderful, lasting gifts. Make some for your friends!

Supplies:

- 32 count linen 8" x 16"
- Weeks Dye Works™ floss – cognac, bright leaf
- Pocket calendar 3 3/4" x 6 3/8" (available at office supply stores)

Directions:

- Cut linen 7" x 15". Zigzag around all 4 sides.

- Fold each end under 1/4" and topstitch.

- **Fold in half.** Press.

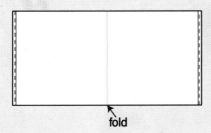

fold

- Turn the linen to the **right** side.

- **Measure** over to the right of the fold 1" and down from the top 1 1/2". Begin the cross stitching at this point.

- Following the chart, cross stitch using one strand of floss.

Cover assembly:

- Place the linen **right side up** on your ironing board.

- From the center fold, **measure 3 7/8"** to the right and the left. Place a pin at each point. This will be the edge of the book cover.

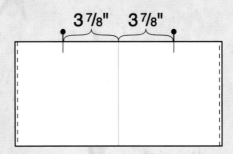

3 7/8"   3 7/8"

- **Fold the sides inward** toward the center fold, stopping at these pins.

• Pin in place – top and bottom.

• Sew a **scant** 1/4" seam all the way across the top and the bottom.

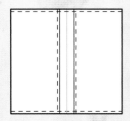

• **Turn right side out**, taking care to make the corners and edges neat. Press.

• Slip your calendar inside.

Cherié Ralston

At an entertainment spot in Gerlach, Nevada, stars lure in the crowds.

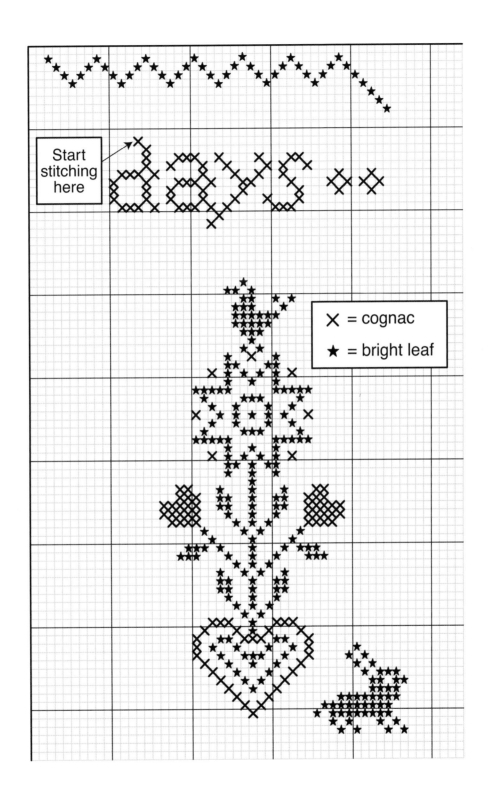

Start stitching here

✕ = cognac

★ = bright leaf

CELIE'S THREAD KEEP

CHAPTER 15

CELIE'S THREAD KEEP

My friend Alma Allen taught me how to paint and wax boxes this way. They can be used for all sorts of things, including gift giving. I use this little sewing box to hold my punchneedle supplies. Your needles, a small hoop, floss and scissors will fit inside perfectly.

Supplies:

- Paper mache' craft box - 7" across x 3" tall
- Folk Art™ acrylic paint – Apple Spice (red), Wrought Iron (black), Teddy Bear Tan (gold)
- 2" or 3" foam paint brush or bristle brush
- 2 - size 8 stencil brushes
- Mylar™ or freezer paper
- Xacto™ knife
- 1/4" hole punch
- Low tack 1" painters tape
- 220 sandpaper
- Light brown Briwax™
- 0000 steel wool

This box is designed to look old – so perfect painting is not necessary!

Directions:

- **Paint** the entire outside of the box (bottom and lid). I used a black, Wrought Iron. Set aside to dry.

- Using Mylar™ or freezer paper, **cut out** the 2 separate stencils (leaf/tulip and star) with an xacto knife.

- To make the **band of dots**, cut a strip of Mylar™ or freezer paper 1" x 8". Place a mark down the center length every 1". Punch holes with the hole punch centering the hole on the marks you have made. (Fig. 1)

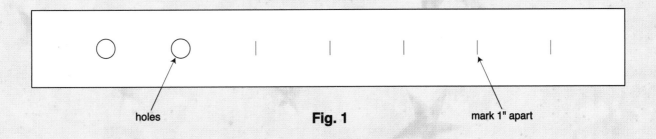

holes   **Fig. 1**   mark 1" apart

- Once the box is dry, run painters tape around the **bottom edge** of the box, lining up one edge of the tape with the bottom edge of the box.

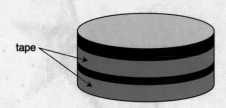

tape

Fig. 2

- From the top edge of that tape, **measure up 3/8"** and make a mark every 3 or 4" around the entire circumference of the box. Run a second line of tape around the entire box lining up the edge of the tape with those marks.

- **Paint this strip red**. Remove the tape. The tape may take off some of the black paint. Don't worry. This will add to the aged look.

- **Stencil** the band of dots using the gold paint. Move the stencil along until you have stenciled all the way around. You may have to space out the last few dots to make them fit. *(Remember: this is folk art — it doesn't have to be perfect!)*

- **Center the leaf/tulip stencil**. Stencil, using the tan paint. Remove the stencil.

- Position the **star stencil**. Stencil with the red paint. Remove the stencil. Let dry a few minutes.

- Lightly **sand the box** and lid. Apply more pressure in a few spots to give it a worn look. Wipe clean.

- **Wax** the outside of the box and lid with the light brown Briwax™. Let it dry for 1/2 hour. Buff with 0000 steel wool.

- Fill your new box with your sewing or punchneedle supplies.

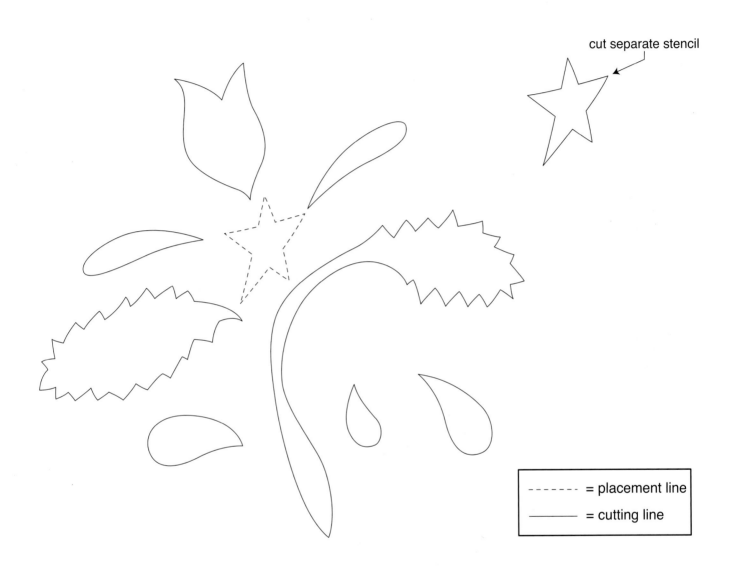

cut separate stencil

- - - - - = placement line
———— = cutting line

CHAPTER 16

HOW TO INVISIBLE MACHINE APPLIQUÉ

The invisible machine appliqué technique is the only way I appliqué. I love appliqué designs, but I could never finish all the appliqué quilts I wanted to by hand because I'm hampered by arthritis. I find this is a painless way to achieve a hand appliqué look.

Basic instructions for this technique follow. For more detailed explanations of different techniques, consult the *Quiltmaker's Guide to Fine Machine Appliqué* by Karla Menaugh and Cherié Ralston from Sunflower Pattern Co-operative (see source list at the end of book).

Supplies needed:

- Sewing machine with zigzag/blind hem capabilities
- Open toe sewing machine foot
- DMC™ 50, Mettler™ 60/2, or Aurifil™ 50 cotton machine embroidery thread
- Freezer paper
- Water soluble glue stick– such as UHU™
- Roxanne's Glue Baste-it™
- Paper scissors, fabric scissors
- Mechanical pencil, fine point permanent pen
- 70/10 denim sewing machine needles
- Iron

Preparing the freezer paper:

You need a freezer paper pattern for each piece you appliqué. There are several ways to make the paper pattern pieces.

- **Tracing:** If you want to trace the pattern piece onto the freezer paper, remember to trace onto the shiny side or your pattern will be reversed. Use a permanent pen for tracing.

- **Templates:** If you are making more than one block, you can make plastic templates to use for tracing pattern pieces.

- **Tacking pattern to freezer paper:** You can stack up to 4 sheets of freezer paper, shiny side up. Place the paper pattern on top and tack all the sheets together in several places with the tip of your iron.

Preparing the fabric:

- *Pre-wash all fabric!* After you have cut out the paper patterns, iron **the *shiny* side** of the freezer paper to the ***wrong side* of the fabric,** allowing about 1/2" between pieces. Cut them out, adding about 3/16" seam allowance around each shape. If the freezer paper should come loose, just touch it with the iron again. **Clip only the inside**

curves. Try not to cut to the very edge of the paper. Get close though!

Gluing:

- With the appliqué piece paper side up, run the glue stick on the fabric, along the edge of the freezer paper. **Apply glue** about 3 inches at a time. Start folding the fabric over the edge of the freezer paper. Use the pad of your thumb or finger. Try to make this **as smooth as possible**. If you have a severe V-shaped curve, push and roll this area so no raw edges show. To get a really smooth edge, use the tip of a seam ripper, stiletto or mechanical pencil to manipulate the fabric while it is still wet with glue. If your fingers get sticky, use a wet paper towel to clean up.

- If the appliqué piece has a point (such as with a leaf, star etc.) **fold the tip in first,** followed by the sides. You don't have to turn under seam allowances that will be overlapped by other appliqué pieces.

Machine set up:

- Use the **same thread** in the bobbin that is used on the top of the machine. If you have a machine that has a bobbin case with a finger that can be threaded (Bernina), thread this also. This keeps the thread pulled to the back of your work.

- Adjust your machine for a **short, narrow overlock stitch** or a blind hem stitch. If you don't have either of these you can use a narrow, fairly open zigzag stitch. *Always practice on a scrap of fabric before stitching your block.*

Stitching:

- With Roxanne's Glue Baste-it™, **glue the appliqué piece**s to your background. Begin stitching, sewing right next to the edge of the appliqué piece. The straight stitches of the over lock stitch should go into the background. The **"bite"** of the stitch should just catch the edge of the appliqué piece. Stitches should less than 1/8" apart. Back stitch a few stitches at the beginning and end.

_�_

- If you have a flower that is layered, **stitch those layers** together first and cut out the back before stitching them to the background.

- After all of the pieces have been stitched down, turn the block over to **trim away the background fabric** under the appliqué. Trim to about a 1/4" seam allowance.

To remove the paper:

- **Submerge** the appliquéd block in water for 30 to 60 seconds. Squeeze out excess water. **Gently pull** the block on the diagonal to release the paper. Quickly **pull out** the paper. Rinse the block in clean water, and roll it in a towel to remove the excess water. Throw your block in the dryer with a couple of dry towels. You need to **dry your block as quickly as possible** to prevent any colors from bleeding. Press with a steam iron from the back.

CHAPTER 17

HOW TO MAKE SETTING TRIANGLES

Don't be afraid of simple math. I follow this easy formula to make setting triangles for a quilt with blocks set on point. Here are formulas for determining the correct sizes of squares to cut.

Corner triangles

How to make half-square triangles with the straight of grain on the 2 short sides.

- To determine the size of the square to cut, **divide the finished block size** by 1.414. Add .875 for the seam allowance and round up to the nearest 1/8".

- **Example**: A 10" finished block divided by 1.414 = 7.072 + .875 = 7.947. Round up to 8". Cut the square 8", and then cut in half diagonally. This will yield 2 corner triangles.

Side triangles

How to make quarter-square triangles with the straight of grain on the long side.

- To determine the size of the square to cut, **multiply the finished block size** by 1.414. Add 1.25 for the seam allowance and round up to the nearest 1/8".

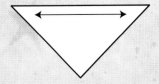

- **Example**: A 10" finished block multiplied by 1.414 = 14.14 + 1.25 = 15.39. Round this up to 15 1/2". Cut your square 15 1/2" and then cut in quarters diagonally. This will yield 4 side triangles.

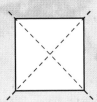 

Fraction to decimal conversions

Below are fraction-to-decimal conversions to help you as you round up numbers.

1/8" = .125
1/4" = .25
3/8" = .375
1/2" = .5
5/8" = .625
3/4" = .75
7/8" = .875

CHAPTER 18

MAKING HALF SQUARE TRIANGLES (SAWTEETH) USING THE GRID SHEET METHOD

This is a quick method for making a lot of sawtooth squares. It's a handy trick to have in your quilter's tool kit!

This grid sheet method uses **2 fabrics**, 1 light and 1 dark to make multiple half square triangle units. **Mark a grid on the lighter fabric** with diagonal lines drawn through the squares. Place the fabrics with **right sides together.** **Stitch a seam** 1/4" on each side of the drawn diagonal line. **Cut apart** the triangles on all drawn lines.

• For manageability, cut 2 pieces of fabric **no larger than 18" x 22"** (fat quarter). Cut one dark and one light.

• Starting at least 1/2" from the raw edge of the light fabric, **draw a grid** of squares on the **wrong side** of the fabric using a fine point pencil or water proof pen. Continue checking the placement of your ruler to **make sure the lines are square and true.**

- Once your grid is drawn, **draw the diagonal lines**. (Fig 1)

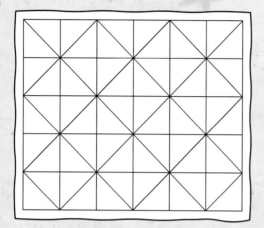

Fig. 1

- Layer the fabrics **right sides together** and steam press. This will hold the fabrics together. Add pins in a few places.

- **Sew** 1/4" on each side of the diagonal lines, as shown. (Fig. 2)

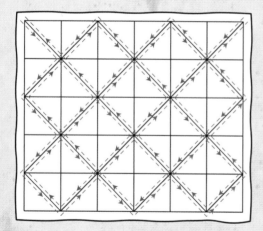

Fig. 2

- **Cut apart** on all drawn lines. (Fig. 3)

Fig. 3

- **Press open** toward the darker fabric and trim points. (Fig. 4)

Fig. 4

To determine the size of the squares you need to draw, **take the finished size of the triangle units and add 7/8"**. For example: if you need 2" finished triangle units — 2" + 7/8" = 2 7/8". Each square you draw will yield 2 half square triangles.

CHAPTER 19

HOW TO COVER ANY BOOK

- **Measure the height** of the book (A, Fig. 1). Add 5/8" seam allowance to this measurement.

- **Measure the width** of the book front, spine and back (B, Fig. 1).

- Measure the width of the **inside** front and back of the book (C and D, Fig. 2).

- Now **add** the B, C and D measurement together (no seam allowance added).

- **Cut the fabric** A plus 5/8" (height) by the total of B, C and D (width).

Inside

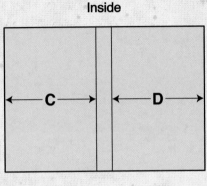

Fig 2

- **Fold under edge**s 1/4" twice and **topstitch**. (E, Fig. 3)

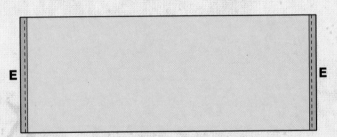

Fig 3

- Now **fold in half** to find the center.

- Pin or **mark the center** at the top and bottom (F, Fig. 4).

Outside

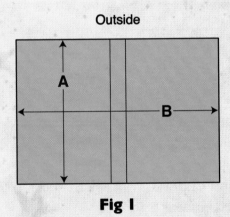

Fig 1

- Open and **lay flat**, right side up.

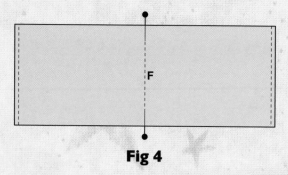

Fig 4

- Take the **outside measurement** (B in Fig. 1) of the book and divide by two.

- Measure **from the center fold out** to that measurement on both sides. Pin or mark at that point on the top and bottom (G, Fig. 5).

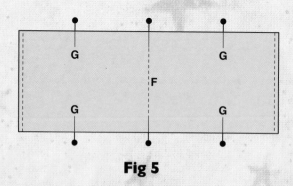

Fig 5

- **Fold the edges** toward the center, stopping at these marks (G, Fig. 6).

- Now **measure** the space left between the two hemmed edges (H, Fig. 7). Add 2" to this measurement.

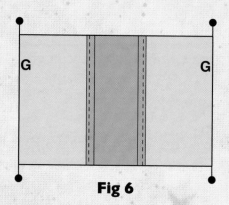

Fig 6

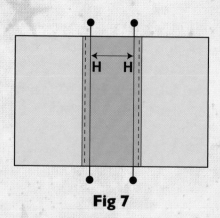

Fig 7

- **Cut 2 strips** of fabric 2" wide by the above measurement.

- **Lay strips in place** right sides down at the top and bottom. (I, Fig. 8)

- **Stitch** 1/4" from the top and the bottom edge to form the book cover. (Fig. 8)

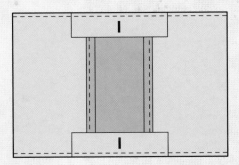

Fig 8

- Turn the book cover **inside out**, making sure the corners are neat. Slip the book into the fabric cover.

The cover design of this book published in 1891 inspired Cherié's Harvest Sun border design.

SOURCES

Tools and notions:
Triangles on a Roll™
Available at local quilt shops
www.trianglesonaroll.com

Add-a-Quarter™
6" Ruler
Available at local quilt shops

Birdhouse Enterprises
Igolochkoy Russian Punchneedle
Gail Bird
Phone: 916-452-5212
Fax: 916-452-1212
www.gailbird.com

CTR, Inc. ™
Punchneedles
Ctrneedleworks.com (will list a store near you)

Timeless Totes™
Colonial Crafts
479 Main Street, Rt 20
Sturbridge, MA 01566
Phone: 800-966-5524
www.colonialcrafts.com

Clover™ notions
Available at local quilt shops

Thread sources:
DMC™
Machine embroidery thread

Herrschners Inc.
www.herrschners.com

Aunt Lenies Attic
365 Beverly Drive
Jefferson, OH 44047
Phone 440-576-4324
email: csdeems@suite224.net

The Quilted Bear
4867 Delta Street
Ladner, BC V4K 2T9
Canada
604-940-7051
www.quiltedbear.net

Aurifil Thread
Machine embroidery thread

That Thread Shop
P.O. Box 325
Lemont II 60439
Phone: 708-301-3172
www.thatthreadshop.com

Weeks Dye Works™
Available at needlework shops
www.weeksdyeworks.com

Wool:
Backyard Quilts
Lisa Bonegean
1713 Northridge Ct.
Menasha, WI 54952
www.backyardquilts.com

Simple Folk
PO Box 509
Sutton, MA 01590
www.simplefolk.com
508-581-8724

Blackberry Primitives
1944 High Street
Lincoln, NE 68502
Cindi 402-423-8464
Tonja 402-421-1361
www.blackberryprimitives.com

Wooly Woolens
Janice Johnson
3107 S. Owens School Rd.
Independence, MO 64057
816-229-2189
Fax 816-229-4145

Books:
Quiltmaker's Guide to Fine Machine Appliqué
By Karla Menaugh and Cherié Ralston
Sunflower Pattern Co-operative
5103 McGregor Dr.
La Grange, KY 40031
502-222-2119
kcmenaugh@sunflower.com

Blackbird Designs
Small Offerings from the Prairie
By Alma Allen and Barb Adams
For general rug hooking instructions
dma@sound.net
www.blackbird-design.com

Linen and frames:
Old Mill Stitchery
Barb Cohee & Mary Atherton
Corbin Mill Place
131 S. Water St.
Liberty, MO 64068
816-792-3670
oldmillstitchery@aol.com